United States Marine Corps
Command and Staff College
Marine Corps University
2076 South Street
Marine Corps Combat Development Command
Quantico, Virginia 22134-5068

Uncharted Waters: Expeditionary Operations and the Naval Component of Union Military Strategy April 1861 to April 1862

SUBMITTED IN PARTIAL FULFILLMENT
OF THE REQUIREMENTS FOR THE DEGREE OF
MASTER OF MILITARY STUDIES

Major Daniel T. Canfield, USMC

March 2008

AY 07-08

Richard L. DiNardo, Ph.D.
Professor of National Security Affairs
Mentor and Oral Defense Committee Member

Paul D. Gelpi, Ph.D.
Associate Professor of Military History
Oral Defense Committee Member

DISCLAIMER

THE OPINIONS AND CONCLUSIONS EXPRESSED HEREIN ARE THOSE OF THE INDIVIDUAL STUDENT AUTHOR AND DO NOT NECESSARILY REPRESENT THE VIEWS OF EITHER THE MARINE CORPS COMMAND AND STAFF COLLEGE OR ANY OTHER GOVERNMENTAL AGENCY. REFERENCES TO THIS STUDY SHOULD INCLUDE THE FOREGOING STATEMENT.

QUOTATION FROM, ABSTRACTION FROM, OR REPRODUCTION OF ALL OR ANY PART OF THIS DOCUMENT IS PERMITTED PROVIDED PROPER ACKNOWLEDGEMENT IS MADE.

Preface

The role of the navy languishes among the most neglected aspects of northern strategic planning. Beyond perfunctory consideration of how the blockade figured in Winfield Scott's Anaconda Plan, most discussions of northern strategy virtually ignore its naval component. In light of the absence of a modern, manuscript-based study of the United States Navy during the Civil War, it should not be surprising, though it is lamentable, that no historian has written a specialized study about Union strategist and the navy.

                                                            Dr. Gary W. Gallagher

A detailed examination of the historiography of the American Civil War reveals a surprising paucity of literature devoted to the initial development of Union military strategy. While most historians generally restrict their work to either land-based studies or further confine themselves almost exclusively to the blue waters of the blockade, the reality is that no objective evaluation of the war can afford to segregate itself in such a manner.

Like most students interested in the military aspects of the conflict, I initially focused my attention on the principal historical actors and events associated with the wars major land battles and campaigns. However, as my research expanded, it also evolved. Significant evidence began to accumulate that challenged many of my previously held assumptions about how the war was fought and conducted. In addition to broadening my perspective, the research associated with this project has dramatically altered the way I think about the war. It may have the potential to do so for others, as well.

In the spring of 1861, the Confederacy possessed just ten ports with internal rail connections to the country's vast interior. Of these, only Mobile, Charleston, and Wilmington were still in Confederate hands by April 1862. The fact that Union forces seized, or otherwise controlled, these crucial strategic locations, just ten months after Bull Run, appeared to be an under-appreciated historical reality that warranted further examination.

In the beginning, I had no particular thesis to prove or disprove, only a professional curiosity about why it took the Union so long to complete a job that it had initially undertaken with such alacrity. This curiosity became even more pronounced when research associated with the blockade not only confirmed its porosity, but actually pointed to something more significant. Given the South's almost total dependence on blockade running to equip and sustain its armed forces, the Union almost certainly missed an opportunity to end war sooner, and at substantially lower cost, if it had only managed to seize one or both of the relatively undefended coastal ports cities of Wilmington and Charleston earlier in the war.

This counterfactual argument eventually expanded into a larger examination of the development of Union military strategy under the direction of Dr. Joseph Glatthaar at the University of North Carolina. Unfortunately, the original thesis became hopelessly diluted within the body of a greatly expanded narrative that focused on a disparate and much more sublime argument. I am particularly grateful to the Marine Corps Command and Staff College and my MMS mentor, Dr. Richard DiNardo, for affording me the opportunity to utilize a portion of the research and writing associated with this former project as a basis to further refine my thoughts and coalesce the original counterfactual argument associated with, in my view, the untapped and underappreciated role of Union combined or expeditionary operations during the first year of the war.

No piece of writing is ever the province of a single individual. This is particularly true with this paper, the research and writing of which, in one form or another, has spanned nearly three years. My military faculty adviser, Colonel Curtis Anderson (USA) and my friends and colleagues in conference group two made the academic year both extremely enlightening and enjoyable. Professors Bruce Bechtol and Mark Jacobsen were simply magnificent and contributed immeasurably to my professional and intellectual growth. I am especially indebted, however, to Professor Richard DiNardo who gave amiably of his time to review the manuscript on several occasions. His sage advice and keen editorial eye saved me from many an embarrassing error and significantly enhanced the quality of scholarship herein. Professor John Gordon also provided quality mentorship and guidance, despite the demands of a busy schedule, and inspired me with his powerful intellect, professionalism, and ideas about expeditionary warfare. Though I have benefited greatly from the benevolent assistance of the aforementioned, any errors of omission, content, or interpretation, rest with the author alone.

My wife Stephanie also deserves special mention. Her patient support and steadfast encouragement have not only sustained me through fifteen years of demanding service, but also proved instrumental in the research and writing associated with this project. Finally, my beautiful and entertaining young children Thomas, Elizabeth, and Daniel serve as a constant source of inspiration. Though at times, I would have certainly preferred a little more tranquility in the early morning or late night hours when I was attempting to organize my thoughts or otherwise compose this paper, they have, in the end, provided the most valuable and enduring contribution to it. Perspective about what is really important in life.

ABSTRACT

Title: Uncharted Waters: Expeditionary Operations and the Naval Component of Union Military Strategy April 1861 to April 1862

Author: Daniel T. Canfield, Major, United States Marine Corps

Background: This paper traces the inception, design, and conduct of Union expeditionary operations during the first year of the war. It focuses on three historical questions. First, was there ever a plan to fully integrate the operational capabilities of the United States Navy into the overall strategic design? Second, was the Confederacy's coastline vulnerable, and would the seizure of specific Southern ports (i.e. Charleston and Wilmington), have been realistic and militarily feasible options capable of being undertaken within the context of the larger Union war effort? Third, what effect, if any, would the seizure of Charleston and/or Wilmington, earlier in the war, had on the Confederacy's ability to resist?

Thesis: The Union missed an opportunity to develop and implement an effective maritime-based strategy during the first year of the war that had the potential to circumvent the costly war of annihilation that eventually unfolded.

Conclusion: Though generally viewed as a land centric struggle, the Civil War still has a great deal to teach us about the potential and enduring relevance of expeditionary power projection, inter-service cooperation, and the imperative of developing and implementing sound military strategy. In the spring of 1861, the Confederacy possessed just ten ports with internal rail connections to the country's vast interior. Of these, only Mobile, Charleston, and Wilmington were still in Confederate hands by April 1862. Throughout the war vast amounts of small arms, saltpeter, meat, and iron flowed through the blockade and poured into the coastal ports of Wilmington and Charleston. These supplies, essential to the Confederate war effort, constituted the South's preeminent strategic vulnerability. The Confederacy, despite Herculean efforts, never came close to establishing the levels of domestic production necessary to wane itself off of its almost total dependence on foreign supply.

Throughout the war, the Union continually attempted to seek a decisive battle in the wrong theater, at the wrong time, against the wrong enemy. The Confederacy's coast was vulnerable. Expeditionary operations to seize the remaining Southern ports and project power further inland were viable military options, which Northern leaders knew of early in the war. The real reasons large-scale expeditionary operations were never undertaken had less to do with technological limitations, poor inter-service cooperation, or a paucity of institutional experience, but, in fact, were rooted in something much more sublime. The Union high commands inability to develop and implement a proper plan for victory.

America remains a sea fearing nation. Although it touts itself as the worlds only super power it may be helpful to temper such self-promoting rhetoric with a realistic assessment of where the nexus of that power really lies. The United States has never been, nor is it currently, particularly well suited or even capable of exercising its national military power in a protracted land-based contest. The Civil War, by far America's bloodiest conflict, serves as a haunting reminder of what can happen when a sea faring nation decides to adopt a continental military strategy.

TABLE OF CONTENTS

	Page
Disclaimer	ii
Preface	iii
Abstract	v
List of Figures	vii
Introduction	1
Background	2
Thesis	2
Anaconda: The Foundation of Union Strategy	3
The Blockade Board and the Inception of an Expeditionary Strategy	5
Hatteras: The Magnificent Distraction	8
The Scott McClellan Feud	10
Port Royal: A Missed Opportunity	12
Conclusion	18

Bibliography

Primary Sources	23
Biographies	24
Secondary Sources	25
Published Articles	30

Appendices

Appendix A: Scott to McClellan (Anaconda Plan)	32
Appendix B: The Blockade Board's Second Report	33
Appendix C: McClellan to Lincoln, 2 Aug. 1861	40

Endnotes	43

LIST OF FIGURES

Page

1. Major Expeditionary Operations of the American Civil War 53

REPORT DOCUMENTATION PAGE	FORM APPROVED - - - OMB NO. 0704-0188

PUBLIC REPORTING BURDEN FOR THIS COLLECTION OF INFORMATION IS ESTIMATED TO AVERAGE 1 HOUR PER RESPONSE, INCLUDING THE TIME FOR REVIEWING INSTRUCTIONS, SEARCHING EXISTING DATA SOURCES, GATHERING AND MAINTAINING THE DATA NEEDED, AND COMPLETING AND REVIEWING THE COLLECTION OF INFORMATION. SEND COMMENTS REGARDING THIS BURDEN ESTIMATE OR ANY OTHER ASPECT OF THIS COLLECTION OF INFORMATION, INCLUDING SUGGESTIONS FOR REDUCING THIS BURDEN, TO WASHINGTON HEADQUARTERS SERVICES, DIRECTORATE FOR INFORMATION OPERATIONS AND REPORTS, 1215 JEFFERSON DAVIS HIGHWAY, SUITE 1204, ARLINGTON, VA 22202-4302, AND TO THE OFFICE OF MANAGEMENT AND BUDGET, PAPERWORK REDUCTION PROJECT (0704-0188) WASHINGTON, DC 20503

1. AGENCY USE ONLY (LEAVE BLANK)	2. REPORT DATE	3. REPORT TYPE AND DATES COVERED STUDENT RESEARCH PAPER

4. TITLE AND SUBTITLE Uncharted Waters: Expeditionary Operations and the Naval Component of Union Military Strategy April 1861 to April 1862	5. FUNDING NUMBERS N/A

6. AUTHOR(S)

DANIEL T. CANFIELD

7. PERFORMING ORGANIZATION NAME(S) AND ADDRESS(ES) USMC COMMAND AND STAFF COLLEGE 2076 SOUTH STREET, MCCDC, QUANTICO, VA 22134-5068	8. PERFORMING ORGANIZATION REPORT NUMBER NONE

9. SPONSORING/MONITORING AGENCY NAME(S) AND ADDRESS(ES) SAME AS #7.	10. SPONSORING/MONITORING AGENCY REPORT NUMBER: NONE

11. SUPPLEMENTARY NOTES

NONE

12A. DISTRIBUTION/AVAILABILITY STATEMENT NO RESTRICTIONS	12B. DISTRIBUTION CODE N/A

ABSTRACT (MAXIMUM 200 WORDS)

The Union missed an opportunity to develop and implement an effective maritime-based strategy during the first year of the war that had the potential to circumvent the costly war of annihilation that eventually unfolded. Throughout the war, the Union continually attempted to seek a decisive battle in the wrong theater, at the wrong time, against the wrong enemy. The Confederacy's coast was vulnerable. Expeditionary operations to seize the remaining Southern ports and project power further inland were viable military options, which Northern leaders knew of early in the war. The real reasons large-scale expeditionary operations were never undertaken had less to do with technological limitations, poor inter-service cooperation, or a paucity of institutional experience, but, in fact, were rooted in something much more sublime. The Union high commands inability to develop and implement a proper plan for victory.

14. SUBJECT TERMS (KEY WORDS ON WHICH TO PERFORM SEARCH) American Civil War; Union Military Strategy; Expeditionary Operations	15. NUMBER OF PAGES: 53
	16. PRICE CODE: N/A

17. SECURITY CLASSIFICATION OF REPORT UNCLASSIFIED	18. SECURITY CLASSIFICATION OF THIS PAGE: UNCLASSIFIED	19. SECURITY CLASSIFICATION OF ABSTRACT UNCLASSIFIED	20. LIMITATION OF ABSTRACT

"A Military, Naval, Littoral War, when wisely prepared and discreetly conducted, is a terrible Sort of War. Happy for that People who are Sovereigns enough of the Sea to put it into Execution! For it comes like Thunder and lightning to some unprepared Part of the World."

—Thomas More Molyneux, 1759

Introduction: On November 7, 1861, a powerful expeditionary force under the command of Flag Officer Samuel Francis Du Pont descended like a thunderclap on the unsuspecting defenders of Forts Walker and Beauregard, guarding the entrance to Port Royal Sound, South Carolina. Union forces captured the strategically located harbor with surprising speed, and at little cost. Just two days later, Du Pont described the operations unexpected success.

> You can form no idea of the terror we have spread in the whole Southern country. Beaufort is deserted; the gunboats were up yesterday to save the light vessels but they were burned the moment the forts surrendered, or rather were destroyed, for the enemy flew in panic leaving public and private property, letters, portfolios, all their regimental achieves, clothes, arms, etc.-they were grandly supplied, ammunition of the most perfect kind, etc. The contrabands are *wild* and sacking Beaufort, in return for being shot down because they would not leave with their masters. [1]

Port Royal was a tremendous accomplishment for Northern arms. Less than six months after Bull Run, the Union placed 12,000 troops on the doorstep of Charleston and Savannah, two of the South's most economically and politically important cities. But while the Navy Department issued congratulatory orders and basked in the warm afterglow of public praise that followed the bold assault, the element of strategic surprise and the advantageous operational position on the South Carolina coast was frittered away by inaction and a lack of imagination.[2] Instead of rapidly exploiting its stunning success further inland, Du Pont's expeditionary force ostensibly spent the next six months trying to figure out what to do next. In the process, the Union squandered a great opportunity to seize the crucial port city of Charleston, early in the war.

Background: In the spring of 1861, the Confederacy possessed just ten ports with internal rail connections to the country's vast interior. Of these, only Mobile, Charleston, and Wilmington remained in Confederate hands by April 1862.[3] The Union, however, failed to seize the remaining southern ports until late in the war. Why did it take the Union so long to complete a job it originally undertook with such alacrity? The subject has received scant historical attention. Rowanna Reed's, *Combined Operations in the Civil War*, remains the only scholarly examination of amphibious operations, and there is still no comprehensive study that places the planning and conduct of naval operations within the larger context of the development and implementation of Union military strategy.[4]

Historical consensus, however, exists on three important points. First, the Union enjoyed unrivaled command of the sea and an overwhelming advantage in strategic mobility. Second, the Confederacy, heavily dependent on the importation of war material throughout the conflict, was almost totally devoid of the natural resources and manufacturing capacity necessary to make war on a large scale. Third, despite the Herculean efforts of the Union Navy, the blockade remained porous until the seizure of Wilmington in January 1865.[5] What remains unclear, however, is why Union authorities consistently pursued the ghost of Napoleon in Virginia, rather than capitalizing on the potential of expeditionary operations to seize southern ports. Was there an alternative military strategy available, or was the conflict irrepressibly destined to degenerate into the land centric, total war of annihilation, it eventually became?

Thesis: This paper's principal argument is that the Union missed an opportunity to develop and implement an effective maritime-based strategy during the first year of the war that had the potential to circumvent the costly war of annihilation that eventually unfolded. It contends that the real reason large-scale expeditionary operations were never undertaken had less to do with technological limitations, poor inter-service cooperation, or a paucity of institutional experience, but, in fact, were rooted in something much more sublime. The Union high commands inability to develop and implement a proper plan for victory.

Anaconda: The Foundation of Union Strategy: Winfield Scott's famous letter to George B. McClellan on May 3, 1861 succinctly conveyed the essential elements of the "Anaconda Plan." Scott's principal strategic objective was to isolate the Confederacy by seizing control of the Mississippi, in combination with a naval blockade (See Appendix A). He envisioned a drive down the Mississippi River Valley no earlier than November of 1861.[6] While this reflected a common sense desire to avoid the perils of disease, it also bought time for Union forces to assemble and prepare. Scott was acutely aware, however, that the greatest danger to his strategic designs lay not from the enemy, but from "the impatience of our patriotic and loyal Union friends" who would "urge instant vigorous action, regardless, I fear, of consequences-that is, unwilling to wait for the slow instruction of (say) twelve or fifteen camps, for the rise of rivers, and the return of frosts to kill the virus of malignant fevers below Memphis."[7] Despite Scott's vast military experience and iconic status, his strategic concept remained unpopular with a large number of political elite in Washington, including the Secretary of the Navy, Gideon Welles, who later wrote "I had in the early stages of the war, disapproved of the policy of General Scott, which was purely defensive,- non intercourse with the insurgents, shut them out from the world by blockade and military frontier lines, but not to invade their territory. The anaconda policy was, I then thought and still think, unwise for the country."[8]

Welles's harbored a fundamentally different view of the strategic situation. In discussing the initial formulation of Union military strategy with Welles, General Joseph Mansfield

(USA), opined that "we must establish our military lines; frontiers between the belligerents as between the countries of continental Europe." The Secretary, clearly uncomfortable with this approach from the beginning, believed both Mansfield's and the army's larger strategic ideas were directly attributable to the myopic teachings of West Point. Which, in turn, were based on a European or, more specifically, a Napoleonic paradigm. Furthermore, Welles believed the implementation of a purely continental strategy inappropriate for conditions in America: "We become by the process rapidly two nations. All beyond the frontiers are considered… as enemies, although large sections and in some instances whole states have a union majority."[9]

Welles's argument, though predicated on dubious political assumptions, nonetheless, reminds us that there were alternative military strategies available to the Union.[10] Welles saw the conflict not as an all out war of annihilation between two opposite and opposing nations, but rather an internal political struggle. He wanted to use expeditionary forces to bolster pro-Union support in selected southern enclaves along the coast. Welles's ideas, however, conflicted with the vast majority of the Army's top leadership, who, at least initially, seemed incapable of conceptualizing a maritime-based strategy that exploited the Confederacy's internal political divisions while simultaneously capitalizing on the Union's superior strategic mobility and potential to project power ashore at a time and place of its choosing.[11]

The Navy, despite Welles's divergent views on grand strategy, moved quickly to support Scott's Anaconda.[12] McClellan's newly created Army of Ohio, then marshalling in Cincinnati, was expected to spearhead the Union's forthcoming drive down the Ohio and Mississippi rivers. The Navy, however, would play an indispensable role. On May 15, 1861, Welles ordered one of his most promising officers, Commander John Rodgers, to report to McClellan's headquarters in Cincinnati, and assist him in the design and implementation of the pending campaign.[13] While supporting Army operations in the Western Theater remained important, the Navy's first strategic priority, in the spring of 1861, was the establishment and maintenance of the blockade.[14] Given the enormity of the southern coastline and the paucity of Union maritime assets, the task appeared foreboding.

The Navy's transition from sail to steam, still far from complete in 1861, further complicated the problem. The challenges of the blockade, already significant, would be magnified considerably if Union steamers had to constantly sally back and forth between Southern ports and distant Northern harbors to replenish their stores. Realizing that a coaling station would have to be seized, but not knowing where, Welles commissioned a four-member board consisting of Professor A. D. Bache, Commander Charles H. Davis, Major John G. Barnard, and Du Pont to examine the issue.[15]

The Blockade Board and the Inception of an Expeditionary Strategy: On June 27, 1861, the board members assembled in professor Bache's office at the Smithsonian.[16] Just eight days later, they published their first report. Though focused on the selection and seizure of a coaling station along the South Atlantic coast, it nonetheless hinted at grander designs. From its inception, the board members distinguished between the seizure of an advanced naval base (i.e. coaling station) for the prosecution of the blockade and the projection of expeditionary combat power ashore in the pursuit of larger strategic and operational objectives.[17] While the board recommended the seizure of Fernandina, Florida, for a variety of tactical considerations, the members emphasized its close proximity to the politically and strategically important cities of Savannah, Charleston, Jacksonville, and Tallahassee. The report concluded with the strong recommendation that the seizure of Fernandina be undertaken in conjunction with a larger operation focused on strategic objectives further inland.[18]

The board released its second report on July 13 (See Appendix B). Unlike the first, it was broader in scope and made a concerted effort to explore the possibility of conducting large-scale, sea-based, expeditionary operations in and around the vicinity of Charleston and Savannah. The board clearly envisioned the strategic potential of an expeditionary operation directed against the Southern coast.[19]

> The putting of 12,000 or 15,000 men thus in the immediate neighborhood of Charleston and Savannah and the presence of a considerable fleet in this noble harbor would doubtless be a sore annoyance to the rebels, and necessitate the constant maintenance of large forces in those cities and on those shores. Yet the same force, naval and military, organized as an expedition and held in hand at New York for a blow anywhere, would threaten not only Savannah and Charleston, but the whole Southern coast.[20]

The board's third report, released on July 16, focused on the complex coastal topography of eastern North Carolina. Realizing that the regions access to the sea was confined to a small number of shallow draft inlets and inland waterways, the board recommended that ten of these crucial channels be obstructed. The plan, in effect, was to simply bottle up the coast in this region. This course of action also had the added benefit of allowing the Union's limited assets (i.e. ships and troops) to be concentrated and employed, in accordance with the board's second report, near the crucial cities of Charleston and Savannah.[21]

On the evening of July 25, the members met with Welles and his assistant secretary, Gustavus Fox, to discuss their reports and recommendations. The strategic situation after Bull Run combined with the impending effects of winter weather on the blockading squadrons lent a sense of urgency to the proceedings. Fox had already informed the President that the Atlantic Blockading Squadron could not remain at sea during the winter months without depots for coal, supplies, and repairs. The board's initial two reports, proposing the seizure of two coaling stations, had already secured a favorable endorsement from the General-in-Chief, and were currently under review in the cabinet. Anticipating the administration's eventual acceptance, the conversation turned to the issues of location and timing.[22]

On August 1, the board members met with General Scott and several key members of his staff. The aged General-in-Chief began the session by first expressing his admiration for the board's work and activities to date. Scott, having already approved of both the necessity and the concept of seizing two coaling stations somewhere along the Confederate coast, had initiated the combined planning conference to work out the details of execution.[23] The General-in-Chief's mature judgment and vast operational experience lent much needed perspective to the deliberations. Though Du Pont originally advocated a landing in late August, Scott's wise counsel quickly convinced him otherwise.[24] It also provided legitimacy and a certain amount of top cover for Du Pont, who now found himself fending off unrealistic expectations from Fox and the Navy Department. Du Pont succinctly summarized both the decision and the subsequent tension it engendered, "it was agreed that the 10th of October instead of the 7th of September was a better day-but the fast people, Fox and Co., are flaring up at what they call delay."[25]

Despite Fox's impetuous displeasure, preparations for the forthcoming operation proceeded at a rapid pace. On August 2, Scott ordered Brigadier General Thomas W. Sherman to "proceed to New York immediately and organize, in connection with Captain Du Pont, of the Navy, an expedition of 12,000 men. Its destination you and the naval commander will determine after you have sailed. You should sail at the earliest possible moment."[26] As subsequent events will illustrate, we are left to merely speculate whether Scott envisioned the pending landing operations to be the forerunner of a larger expeditionary campaign. Yet, given the contents of the widely circulated board reports and Scott's own personal experience with combined operations, it is hard to imagine that the thought of these initial beachheads being used for the introduction of substantial follow on forces did not occur to Scott or the joint planners as they frantically prepared to outfit and embark America's largest expeditionary force since the Mexican War.[27]

Given the board's experience and intellectual abilities, it is not surprising that the members refused to confine themselves to the simple selection of two coaling stations.[28] Du Pont and Davis eventually became interested in transitioning the board's findings into actual operational plans and directives. In late September, Du Pont pleaded with Fox to allow Davis to return to Washington and complete, what he viewed, as the board's most important report.[29] While Du Pont's plea to translate the board reports into actual plans and directives attested to how far the member's role and thinking had evolved, the fact that Fox ignored the request reflected the reality of who was actually calling the shots in Washington.[30]

Hatteras: The Magnificent Distraction: While the board members immersed themselves in the details of the pending Port Royal expedition, Welles's attention momentarily turned to North Carolina. Confederate privateering had long been a source of great embarrassment and concern to the department.[31] On August 12, the New York Board of Underwriters forwarded a collection of reports detailing the plight of several Northern merchantmen that had recently fallen victim to Rebel privateers based in the Outer Banks.[32] Welles, decided to end Confederate privateering off the North Carolina coast and the bad publicity it was generating for the department. On August 13, Scott ordered General Wool, then commanding Union ground forces at Fort Monroe to "prepare a sufficient detachment to accompany an expedition, under Commander Stellwagen, against some batteries on Hatteras Inlet, North Carolina." [33]

Scott viewed the Hatteras expedition as a small and limited objective attack in support of the Navy's effort to bottle up Confederate privateers operating along the North Carolina coast.[34] With preparations now fully underway in support of the pending Port Royal expedition, he did not want, nor did he anticipate, a permanent or substantial commitment of Union ground forces on the North Carolina coast. Wool, however, bristled at what he saw as an over-centralized and under-resourced set of instructions emanating from Washington. On August 24, he wrote the General-in-Chief complaining: "To operate on this coast with success (I mean between this and Florida) we want more troops. At any rate, I think we ought to have a much larger force in this department." Interestingly, Wool, despite being ignorant of the board reports, also envisioned the strategic potential of expeditionary operations to alter the operational situation in Virginia, "If I had 20,000 or 23,000 men, in conjunction with the Navy, we could do much on this coast to bring back from Virginia the troops of North Carolina, South Carolina, and Georgia."[35]

On August 29, 1861, just sixteen days after receiving the initiating directive from Washington, Union forces under Flag Officer S. H. Stringham and General Benjamin F. Butler received the unconditional surrender of the Confederate forces manning Forts Hatteras and Clark.[36] What started out as a distraction, evolved into an important use of combined operations.[37] Though the army played a minimal role in the assault, the operation closed Pamlico Sound to Southern privateers, provided a much-needed boost to Northern moral, and temporarily silenced the Navy Department's critics.[38]

The unexpected ease of the Union's amphibious assault caught both sides by surprise. Though Butler had strict orders not to permanently garrison the forts, he quickly disregarded those instructions once he realized the strategic significance of the position. Both Butler and Stringham clearly envisioned the tremendous opportunity to further Union operational and strategic objectives along the coast and further inland.[39] While Union authorities contemplated their new found opportunities, Southern leaders reacted with disdain and disbelief. The Confederate Congress quickly passed a resolution calling for a detailed accounting of the events surrounding the Hatteras disaster. Shortly thereafter, Jefferson Davis came to the somber conclusion, "Preparations to put the coast of the State of North Carolina in a proper condition for defense are still in progress and will receive such additional attention as this occasion indicates to be necessary."[40]

The Hatteras Expedition demonstrated both the vulnerability of the Southern coastline and the strategic potential for expeditionary operations to exploit internal political divisions within the Confederacy. Many Southerners feared the surprise assault at Hatteras foreshadowed a larger expeditionary campaign designed to project Union military power further inland.[41] The ominous threat of Union seaborne expeditionary operations forced many Southern law makers to ponder the vulnerability of their respective shores and question the wisdom of sending state raised troops north to defend Richmond.[42] Conceived on the alter of states rights, the Confederacy inherited a cruel choice - defend its new capital and the vital industry it housed or protect the vulnerable coastline of its Southern states. It could not do both. Fortunately for Southern lawmakers, it was a dilemma Union strategy failed to engineer.

The Scott McClellan Feud: While Union authorities contemplated their unexpected success in North Carolina, McClellan's presence in the nation's capital hindered the planning and execution of the Port Royal expedition, and ultimately dictated a complete reversal of Union military strategy. The "Young Napoleon," summoned to Washington in the wake of the Bull Run debacle, assumed command of the newly created Division of the Potomac on July 27.[43] Rather than cooperating with the General-in-Chief, he promptly initiated a nefarious effort to usurp him.[44] On August 2, McClellan submitted his own views on grand strategy directly to the President (See Appendix C).[45]

While Scott's Anaconda correctly anticipated the difficulties associated with prosecuting offensive operations in Virginia and wisely endeavored to avoid them, McClellan's strategic concept actually sought decisive battle in the Commonwealth.[46] McClellan, in effect, advocated a reverse image of Scott's "Anaconda Plan."[47] Destroying Confederate forces then massing in Virginia and the swift capture of Richmond, not a methodical drive down the Mississippi, became the Union's strategic main effort. Expeditionary operations, however, formed an important, albeit supporting, part of McClellan's strategic designs.[48] The young general, however, quickly found himself at odds with Scott and the Navy Department.

McClellan shamelessly lobbied the President to concentrate every available Union asset in Washington, believing that the capital was in "imminent danger."[49] Despite Scott's best efforts to reassure the President otherwise, McClellan's accusations set off a near panic in Lincoln's mind. On September 14, the President, fearing for the safety of the capital, cancelled the Port Royal expedition.[50] While McClellan clearly possessed a conceptual appreciation for expeditionary operations, his actions reflected a certain stubborn self-interest. McClellan's pending move on Richmond and his attempt to gain strategic control of the Union war effort, not any clairvoyant view of Union grand strategy, dictated that any attempt to employ sea borne maneuver at other, more vulnerable, points along the

Confederate coast would have to wait.[51] Welles, however, insisted otherwise. On September 17, he raised the subject of Port Royal with "great spirit" before the cabinet, and convinced the President to rescind his earlier decision canceling the expedition.[52]

The indecision surrounding Port Royal symbolized the confusion inherent in the Union high command during the fall of 1861. Who was actually running military affairs and guiding the strategic direction of the war? Many in Washington felt it was only a matter of time before McClellan, the all too apparent successor to Scott, would formally unseat the General-in-Chief. Scott, however, still admirably attempted to discharge his duties and convince an increasingly impatient and skeptical administration to adhere to the strategic principles of his Anaconda Plan. McClellan's inability to cooperate with Scott, and Lincoln's unwillingness to make him, contributed to the strategic intransigence and adversely affected the operational and strategic direction of the war at a crucial time.

The internal squabbling essentially resulted in a three-month operational pause for the Union war effort. The once promising levels inter-service cooperation, involving none other than Scott, himself, came to a screeching halt as the aged General-in-Chief spent the majority of his time and intellectual energy fending off McClellan and his growing number of critics in Washington. Sadly, the infighting could not have come at a worse time for the Union beachheads on the coast of North and South Carolina. By the time McClellan was formally installed as the Commander of all U.S. armies on November 7, 1861, the reality of winter weather and the disorganization brought about by the dramatic change in leadership and strategic priorities, postponed any offensive action until the spring of 1862.

Port Royal: A Missed Opportunity Despite months of planning, the actual destination of Du Pont's expedition remained undecided.[53] On October 23, the flag officer hosted a joint planning conference with Generals Sherman, Wright, Stevens, and Viele aboard his flagship, the USS *Wabash,* anchored in Hampton Rhoads.[54] After an arduous session that went late into the night, the officers finally decided upon Port Royal early the next morning.[55] Five days latter, on October 29, Du Pont's amphibious task force, comprising fifty vessels and caring over 12,000 troops, finally got underway.[56]

Unlike Hatteras, Confederate reaction to the seizure of Port Royal was swift. Robert E. Lee assumed command of a newly created military department encompassing the vulnerable southeastern coast of the Confederacy.[57] Lee arrived in Charleston on November 7, and immediately embarked upon a hastily arranged inspection tour of his new command.[58] By the end of November, Lee realized he was in a race against time to strengthen his defenses before the Federals seized upon the opportunity to move inland. Concentrating his command's limited assets at those points he felt most important, Lee worked feverishly to shore up his department's inadequate defenses.[59]

In early January, he warned Confederate authorities in Richmond that, "The forces of the enemy are accumulating, and apparently increase faster than ours. I have feared, if handled with proportionate ability with his means of speedy transportation and concentration, it would be impossible to gather troops necessarily posted over a long line in sufficient strength, to oppose sudden movements." Painfully aware of the great tactical dilemma confronting his forces, he further lamented: "Wherever his fleet can be brought no opposition to his landing can be made except within range of our fixed batteries. We have nothing to oppose to its heavy guns, which sweep over the low banks of this country with irresistible force."[60] While Northern leaders vacillated, Lee begrudgingly acknowledged the opportunity available to Union arms: "I have thought his purpose would be to seize upon the Charleston and Savannah Railroad near the head of Broad River, sever the line of communication between those cities with one of his columns of land troops, and with his other two and his fleet by water envelop alternately each of those cities. This would be a difficult combination for us successfully to resist." [61]

Ironically, both Du Pont and Sherman clearly envisioned the same opportunity. [62] On November 15, Du Pont's friend and fellow board member, Henry Davis, tactfully reminded the flag officer:

> Burnside still lingers at Annapolis-as if the government wished Sherman to be driven into the sea before he is reinforced. However I do not think all South Carolina and Georgia can do that. But 50,000 men ought to be sent there, and they could take Charleston and Savannah and penetrate to the Tennessee line and the Mississippi River. I feel sure that when the shell is broken the egg will be found rotten if not empty. [63]

By early December, Du Pont echoed Davis's recommendation, "I would say that the forces should be largely increased and a regular campaign in the South be commenced-say with 50,000 men."[64] With Union gunboats now in a position to support army operations further inland, an increasingly frustrated Du Pont lamented, "Savannah and Charleston must be taken, but it must be done *selon les regles* with a large force. So far we have been cutting at the extremities"[65]

Though Du Pont recognized the opportunity to project Union expeditionary power inland; he also knew Fox and the department expected him to seize and establish a second coaling station at Fernandina, Florida.[66] The capture of Port Royal, however, dictated a reexamination of the expedition's original purpose. Port Royal Sound, when combined with the other interconnected inland waterways, was both deep enough and large enough to serve as an entire fleet anchorage. The Navy did not need a second coaling station or safe harbor. This fact was not lost on Sherman who observed, "It may be hence inferred that the main object of the expedition has been already accomplished, and that the point of Fernandina is now of so secondary a character as to render it not only almost insignificant, but the operation of taking it actually prejudicial to the great work which the development of circumstances appears to have set before us."[67]

On December 14, Sherman wrote to the Army's Adjutant General clearly outlining the strategic opportunity available to Union forces, and bemoaning the political decision to undertake the Fernandina operation: "I am aware of the good effect that the capture of this place would have on the public mind, but the military is the only point of view that should be taken of it. It is no point from which to operate, and will probably fall of itself the moment Savannah is occupied by our forces, and therefore the resources of the Navy and Army here should be husbanded for a more important operation, viz, the attack of the enemy's line the moment preparations can be made."[68] Sherman concluded with a plea for reinforcements, and observed "I am firmly convinced that an operation of this sort would not only give us Savannah, but, if successful and strong enough to follow up time success, would shake the so-called Southern Confederacy to its very foundation."[69]

Fox, however, continued to insist otherwise. On January 4, he wrote a terse letter to Du Pont, urging the flag officer to seize Fernandina as originally planned. While acknowledging Fox's political calculations, Du Pont reminded the Assistant Secretary, "that the original plan of the expedition contemplated the seizure and the occupation of two ports, as harbors of refuge; and that I have taken seven ports, and now actually hold five ports, of which three are in South Carolina, and two in Georgia; and of which five ports, three are held by me in conjunction with the army." [70]

Unfortunately, the immense opportunity along the South Carolina coast occurred at the very moment the Union high command was in complete disarray. McClellan, having finally usurped Scott as General-in-Chief on November 1, was simply unwilling to exploit the strategic situation in Port Royal Sound. As the young general grappled with the complexities and increased responsibilities of his new post, the unprecedented opportunity to seize Charleston, though present and clearly articulated, was neither in line with his reversal of Union military strategy nor his preconceived notions of the way the war needed to unfold.[71] Richmond, not Charleston, reflected McClellan's myopic strategic priorities. Despite a clairvoyant appreciation for amphibious based expeditionary operations, once McClellan actually became General-in-Chief, he found it much easier, and safer, to simply direct all available Union resources to his army, then mustering on the banks of the Potomac.[72]

Sherman spent the winter months erecting fortifications, conducting minor operations, and pleading for reinforcements. As Du Pont so aptly observed, "Sherman's troops were more than ample to occupy the possession here, yet not sufficient to open a campaign between the two largest rebel cities on the Atlantic coast, and no plan had been adopted in reference to one."[73] Public pressure eventually mounted as newspaper articles portrayed a lack of inter-service cooperation and grew increasingly impatient with Sherman's apparent timidity along the coast.[74] Rather than sending reinforcements, McClellan eventually ordered Sherman to detach troops in support of the Fernandina operation, while simultaneously directing him to seize Fort Pulaski guarding the nautical approaches to the Savannah River.[75]

The Union's inability to seize Charleston in late 1861, or early 1862, constituted one of the greatest missed opportunities of the war. Ironically, responsibility for the failure rested in Washington. Fox, perhaps more than McClellan, was the primary catalyst. He pressured Du

Pont to move on Fernandina from the very start. This was done, however, with a view of increasing the Navy Department's "prestige" by capturing yet another coastal city, rather than any sincere effort to further Union strategic objectives. Rather than advocating a combined expeditionary campaign to capture Charleston during the first year of the war, the Assistant Secretary seemed perfectly content to disperse Union expeditionary power in a thin veneer along the coast until enough ironclads could be fielded to take "the cradle of secession" by a naval *coup de main*. While the early seizure of Charleston would have had immense political and psychological ramifications, the real strategic value of the city remained rooted in the Confederacy's principal strategic vulnerability-it was hopelessly dependant on the foreign importation of war material.[76]

Throughout the war, vast amounts of small arms, saltpeter, meat, and iron flowed through the blockade and poured into the coastal ports of Wilmington and Charleston.[77] These supplies, essential to the Confederate war effort, constituted the South's preeminent strategic vulnerability.[78] Despite Herculean efforts to create and organize Southern manufacturing, the Confederacy never manufactured more war material than it imported, and never came close to reaching the levels of domestic production that could have allowed it to survive had the crucial ports of Charleston and Wilmington been taken earlier in the war.[79] The Confederacy's coast was vulnerable. Union leaders knew it. Expeditionary operations to seize these ports and project power further inland were viable military options, capable of being undertaken within the context of the larger Union war effort. Despite capturing or otherwise controlling all but three of the Confederacy's principal seafaring ports by April 1862, Union leaders appeared strangely naïve to the unremarkable realization that the most effective way to implement the blockade was to simply seize the ports.[80]

Conclusion: Given the limited scope of this paper, it would be dangerous to construct a set of too far reaching conclusions. Nonetheless, several intriguing observations appear evident. First, the Confederacy's coastline was vulnerable, and the seizure of specific Southern ports, e.g. Charleston and Wilmington, were realistic and militarily feasible options capable of being undertaken within the context of the larger Union war effort. Second, Federal leaders were cognizant of the former. Third, the South was extremely dependant on the importation of war material, and the seizure of Charleston and Wilmington earlier in the war would have materially altered the strategic situation. Finally, at least during the first year of the war, the operational capabilities of the United States Navy were fully integrated into the larger strategic design of the war.[81]

Although focused on the blockade, the Navy, in accordance with Scott's Anaconda Plan, played a major role in supporting joint operations along the Confederacy's western rivers. Welles also took the unprecedented step of establishing a joint service naval board. Its members produced a series of thoughtful and innovative reports that served as a basis for the employment of Union sea power throughout the war. The board also advocated the creation and employment of large-scale expeditionary forces that were capable of operating both along the coast and further inland in pursuit of strategic objectives. Scott's conference with the members of the naval board on August 1, 1861, concerning the planning and the execution of the Port Royal expedition was an impressive early example of what was possible when the two services came together in pursuit of common strategic objectives.

Despite these impressive examples of inter-service cooperation, a broader analysis of the war, nonetheless, confirms the widely held view that full strategic potential of the Union Navy and combined expeditionary operations, in particular, were never realized. The reasons for this failure, however, appear inextricably linked, not to inferior technology, coastal topography, or the occasional inter departmental squabbling, but to something much more sublime-the Union's inability to develop and implement an effective military strategy.

The strategic intransigence occurred for three reasons. First, with the marginalization of Scott and his subsequent dismissal, the Union's military strategy went from a combined maritime-based policy to one that sought a land-centric victory. Second, while McClellan clearly envisioned the employment of combined operations, limited resources and his own decision to personally seek out and lead the Army of the Potomac in a decisive battle of annihilation in Virginia prevented the implementation of a maritime-based strategy that effectively integrated expeditionary operations within Union grand strategy. Third, the Navy, primarily through the influence and Machiavellian efforts of its Assistant Secretary, Gustavus Fox, habitually displayed a penchant to put the department's interests ahead of the nation's. Though the Navy's principal commanders Du Pont, Stringham, Foote, and Goldsborough, consistently advocated the use of combined operations and cooperation with the Army at the tactical and operational levels, Fox pushed back. The Assistant Secretary sincerely felt, "The Navy must end the war! The Army cannot do it!"[82] Rather than establishing a command climate that fostered and encouraged the attainment of common strategic objectives, he pressured Union naval commanders to make the department's "prestige," their focus of effort.

The Union enjoyed tremendous advantages in almost every category used to calculate military potential. The Confederates, by contrast, were significantly out manned, out gunned, and under supplied. Yet by the summer of 1862, Lee had not only repelled McClellan's assault on Richmond, but had sent Union forces scurrying back into the nation's capital for the second time in as many years. He crossed over the Potomac, and was in a position to win a victory on Northern soil that threatened foreign intervention. How could this be? Was the Southern fighting man superior to his northern cousin? Were the Confederacy's officers simply better than their Northern counterparts? Did the Southerner enjoy a certain moral ascendancy over his Union antagonist? While these theories, no doubt interesting, have sparked their fair share of scholarly discourse, the principal reason Lee was in Maryland was because the Union failed to implement an effective military strategy.

McClellan's reversal of Scott's initial strategic designs unintentionally set the precedent for a long-term commitment of Union forces to a prolonged, bloody, and indecisive war of attrition in the restricted terrain of Virginia. Rather than working with Scott to develop and implement an effective military strategy that exploited Confederate vulnerabilities and calmed the nerves of men like Chase, Wade, Blair, and the other champions of the "On to Richmond" policy, McClellan's duplicity created an aura of false expectations about prompt military action that eventually led to his own downfall.[83] While the destruction of the enemy's principal field army and the capture of Richmond was certainly Clausewitzian, and undoubtedly pleased many in Washington, it was not a smart military strategy. Instead of attacking Confederate weakness, it attacked Southern strength. Instead of seizing a center of gravity, it inadvertently created one.[84]

Perhaps the greatest strategic shortfall in the development of Union military strategy was its failure to employ expeditionary operations along the coast. Northern public opinion and international recognition were the cornerstones of Southern strategy. Both required time. Yet, while the Confederacy needed to prolong the war and win military victories, time was not necessarily on its side. For every battlefield success that theoretically procured more time, it also allowed the ever-tightening economic noose around its neck to further constrict.

This was the great dichotomy of Southern strategy the Union failed to exploit. By disregarding Scott's plan and choosing to prosecute decisive ground combat operations in Virginia, the Lincoln administration implemented a flawed military strategy that actually facilitated Southern war aims. Instead of executing a strategic holding action in the east, the Union continued to bludgeon itself against the best army the Confederacy was capable of producing in a theater that was naturally predisposed to the tactical and operational defense. Thus, the Union, foolishly guided by the combination of McClellan's grandiose visions of martial glory, the impatience of an overzealous Commander-in-Chief, and the vocal admonishments of a small number of radical Republicans, embarked upon a military strategy that came precariously close to giving the South the string of military victories it so desperately needed to erode Northern support and gain international recognition.

Throughout the war, the Union continually attempted to seek a decisive battle in the wrong theater, at the wrong time, against the wrong enemy. The Union was capable of seizing all the Southern ports early in the war. While this would have prevented offensive action in Virginia, it would have been in line with Scott's original strategic thinking, and as certain as any non event in history can be, would likely have crippled the Confederacy before it had a chance to develop its war making infrastructure. The great tactical lesson that emerged from the war was the superiority of the defense. Time after time, whether it was at the Seven Days, Fredericksburg, Gettysburg, Franklin, Cold Harbor, or the Mule Shoe, entrenched defenders consistently decimated attacking formations. If the Union had seized the strategically vital port cities of Charleston, Wilmington, and Mobile earlier in the war, and then erected fortifications and assumed the tactical defense, the course and the cost of the conflict would have been dramatically altered. The Confederacy would have faced a cruel strategic dilemma. Either to assault these fortified bastions or suffer the slow strangulation Winfield Scott's Anaconda Plan had so astutely tried to engineer.

Eventually, the Union destroyed the South through the application of overwhelming military force.[85] Whether this was inevitable or not constitutes an argument significantly beyond the scope of this paper, but as Walter Mills noted:

> Perhaps the most significant thing about this war was the fact that it was not really decided by the armies. There was no "decisive" battle even at Petersburg. The South simply ran out of manpower-rather as Hitler's Germany did in 1945. It was at the same time, of course, running out of much else. It had been cut to pieces by the campaign on the Mississippi and the march through Georgia. Its war industry in Georgia and Alabama had been captured. The blockade had finally become effective; the fall of Fort Fisher on the Cape Fear in 1865 had closed the last outlet to the world. The last firm center of resistance in Virginia had nothing more to stand on. Lee, a Virginia aristocrat, recognized the situation as Hitler, the paranoiac, was never able to do. There was no other possible outcome. But the Army of Northern Virginia had not been defeated; it was surrendered." [86]

With the clairvoyance of hindsight, it seems certain that Lee's army would have been surrendered much earlier had the Union simply seized two of the three Confederate ports that still remained open to the outside world in April 1862. However fortuitous the final outcome of the war looks to us today, we must be careful not to judge the strategic conduct of the conflict through the glasses of twentieth-century Clausewitzian hindsight. Union strategy was flawed, not because it neglected to anticipate and implement the requirements of total war on its own population sooner, but rather, because it failed to develop the necessary military strategy to win a limited one earlier.[87] The tragedy for the Union in the spring of 1862 was not that the flower of American youth lay shriveling on the banks of the Tennessee River at Shiloh or in the marshy battlefields of the Seven Days, but that the group of men the Northern people counted on to both define and secure victory appeared incapable of designing a comprehensive plan to do so.

Primary Sources

Butler, Benjamin F. and Jessie Ames Marshall. *Private and Official Correspondence of Gen. Benjamin F. Butler, during the Period of the Civil War*. Norwood, Mass.: Plimpton Press, 1917.

Du Pont, Samuel Francis. *Official Dispatches and Letters of Rear Admiral Du Pont, U. S. Navy.1846-48. 1861-63*. Wilmington, Del.: Press of Ferris Bros., Printers, 1883.

Du Pont, Samuel Francis, John Daniel Hayes, and Eleutherian Mills Historical Library. *Samuel Francis Du Pont; a Selection from His Civil War Letters*. Ithaca, N.Y.: Published for the Eleutherian Mills Historical Library by Cornell University Press, 1969.

Fox, Gustavus Vasa, Robert Means Thompson, and Louis H. Bolander. *Confidential Correspondence of Gustavus Vasa Fox : Assistant Secretary of the Navy, 1861-1865*. New York: Printed for the Naval history society by De Vinne press, 1918.

Gorgas, Josiah and Frank Everson Vandiver. *The Civil War Diary of General Josiah Gorgas; Ed. by Frank E. Vandiver*. University, Ala: Univ. of Alabama Press, 1947.

Gorgas, Josiah and Sarah Woolfolk Wiggins. *The Journals of Josiah Gorgas, 1857-1878*. Tuscaloosa: University of Alabama Press, 1995.

Hitchcock, Ethan Allen and W. A. Croffut. *Fifty Years in Camp and Field ,Diary of Major- General Ethan Allen Hitchcock, U.S.A*. New York; London: G.P. Putnam's Sons, 1909.

Huse, Caleb. *The Supplies for the Confederate Army, how they were obtained in Europe and how Paid for*. Boston: Press of T.R. Marvin & son, 1904.

Jones, J. B. and Howard Swiggett. *A Rebel War Clerk's Diary at the Confederate States Capital*. A new and enl. , ed. New York: Old Hickory Bookshop, 1935.

Lee, Robert E. and Jefferson Davis. *Lee's Dispatches; Unpublished Letters of General Robert E. Lee, to Jefferson Davis and the War Department of the Confederate States of America, 1862-65. from the Private Collection of Wymberley Jones De Renne, of Wormsloe, Georgia*. New ed. New York: Putnam, 1957.

Lee, Robert E. and Clifford Dowdey. *The Wartime Papers of R.E. Lee*. Virginia Civil War Centennial, 1961-1965. 1st ed. Boston: Little, Brown, 1961.

Lee, Robert Edward and William Taylor Thom. *Recollections and Letters of General Robert E. Lee*. Garden City, N.Y.: Garden City Pub. Co, 1924.

Lincoln, Abraham, Roy Prentice Basler, and Abraham Lincoln Association. *Collected Works of Abraham Lincoln*. New Brunswick, N.J.: Rutgers University Press, 1953.

McClellan, George Brinton and Stephen W. Sears. *The Civil War Papers of George B. McClellan: Selected Correspondence, 1860-1865* [Correspondence.]. New York: Ticknor & Fields, 1989.

Porter, David D. *The Naval History of the Civil War*. Dover ed. Mineola, NY: Dover Publications, 1998.

Rains, George Washington and United Confederate Veterans. *History of the Confederate Powder Works*. Newburgh, N. Y.: Newburgh daily news print, 1882.

Scott, Winfield. *Memoirs of Lieut.-General Scott, LL.D*. Freeport, N.Y: Books for Libraries Press, 1970.

United States. Navy Dept, Richard Rush, and United States. Naval War Records Office. *Official Records of the Union and Confederate Navies in the War of the Rebellion*. Harrisburg, Pa.: National Historical Society : Distributed by Broadfoot Pub. Co., Historical Times, Morningside House, 1987.

United States. War Dept and Robert N. Scott. *The War of the Rebellion : A Compilation of the Official Records of the Union and Confederate Armies*. Harrisburg, PA: National Historical Society, 1971.

Welles, Gideon. *The Papers of Gideon Welles*. Washington, D.C.: Library of Congress Photo duplication Service, 1988.

Welles, Gideon and Edgar Thaddeus Welles. *Diary of Gideon Welles, Secretary of the Navy Under Lincoln and Johnson*. Boston: Houghton Mifflin, 1911.

Biographies

Du Pont, Henry. *Rear-Admiral Samuel Francis Du Pont, United States Navy: A Biography*. New York: National Americana Society, 1926.

Elliott, Charles Winslow. *Winfield Scott, the Soldier and the Man*. New York: The Macmillan Company, 1937.

Freeman, Douglas Southall. *R. E. Lee, a Biography*. New York: Scribner, 1934.

Hassler, Warren W. *General George B. McClellan, Shield of the Union*. 1st ed. Baton Rouge: Louisiana State University Press, 1957.

Johnson, Timothy D. *Winfield Scott : The Quest for Military Glory*. Modern War Studies. Lawrence: University Press of Kansas, 1998.

Macartney, Clarence Edward Noble. *Mr. Lincoln's Admirals*. New York: Funk & Wagnalls Co., 1956.

Merrill, James M. *Du Pont, the Making of an Admiral : A Biography of Samuel Francis Du Pont*. 1st ed. New York, N.Y.: Dodd, Mead, 1986.

Niven, John. *Gideon Welles; Lincoln's Secretary of the Navy*. New York: Oxford University Press, 1973.

Peskin, Allan. *Winfield Scott and the Profession of Arms*. Kent, Ohio: Kent State University Press, 2003.

Rafuse, Ethan Sepp. *McClellan's War: The Failure of Moderation in the Struggle for the Union* 2005.

Sears, Stephen W. *George B. McClellan : The Young Napoleon*. New York: Ticknor & Fields, 1988.

Weddle, Kevin John. *Lincoln's Tragic Admiral : The Life of Samuel Francis Du Pont*. A Nation Divided. Charlottesville: University of Virginia Press, 2005.

West, Richard S. *Gideon Welles, Lincoln's Navy Department*. 1st ed. Indianapolis: Bobbs-Merrill, 1943.

Secondary Sources

Anderson, Bern. *By Sea and by River: The Naval History of the Civil War*. 1st ed. New York: Knopf, 1962.

Barrett, John Gilchrist. *The Civil War in North Carolina*. Chapel Hill: University of North Carolina Press, 1997.

Baxter, James Phinney. *The Introduction of the Ironclad Warship*. Classics of Naval Literature. Classics of naval literature ed. Annapolis, Md.: Naval Institute Press, 2001.

Beatie, Russel Harrison. *Road to Manassas; the Growth of Union Command in the Eastern Theatre from the Fall of Fort Sumter to the First Battle of Bull Run*. 1st ed. New York: Cooper Square Publishers, 1961.

Beringer, Richard E. *Why the South Lost the Civil War*. Athens, Ga.: University of Georgia Press, 1986.

Boaz, Thomas. *Guns for Cotton: England Arms the Confederacy*. Shippensburg, PA, USA: Burd Street Press, 1996.

Browning, Robert M. *Success is all that was Expected: The South Atlantic Blockading Squadron during the Civil War*. 1st ed. Washington, D.C.: Brassey's, Inc., 2002.

———. *From Cape Charles to Cape Fear : The North Atlantic Blockading Squadron during the Civil War*. Tuscaloosa: University of Alabama Press, 1993.

Browning, Robert S. *Two if by Sea : The Development of American Coastal Defense Policy*. Contributions in Military History. Vol. 33. Westport, Conn.: Greenwood Press, 1983.

Burton, E. Milby. *The Siege of Charleston, 1861-1865*. Columbia: University of South Carolina Press, 1970.

Carbone, John Stephen, North Carolina. Division of Archives and History, and Outer Banks History Center. *The Civil War in Coastal North Carolina*. Raleigh, N.C.: Division of Archives and History, North Carolina Department of Cultural Resources, 2001.

Catton, Bruce. *Mr. Lincoln's Army*. Catton, Bruce, 1899-1978. the Army of the Potomac. Vol. 1. Garden City, N.Y.: Doubleday, 1962.

———. *The Centennial History of the Civil War*. E. B. Long, Director of Research. 1st ed. Garden City, N.Y.: Doubleday, 1961.

Corbett, Julian Stafford. *Some Principles of Maritime Strategy /by Julian S. Corbett*. New ed. London; New York: Longmans, Green, 1918.

Davis, William C. *Battle at Bull Run : A History of the First Major Campaign of the Civil War*. Louisiana pbk. ed. Baton Rouge: Louisiana State University Press, 1981.

Donald, David Herbert. *Lincoln Reconsidered : Essays on the Civil War Era*. 3rd , rev. and updat, Vintage Books ed. New York: Vintage Books, 2001.

———. *Why the North Won the Civil War*. Baton Rouge: Louisiana State University Press, 1960.

Dufour, Charles L. and Carolyn A. Wallace. *The Night the War was Lost*. 1st ed. Garden City, N.Y.: Doubleday, 1960.

Earle, Edward Mead, Gordon Alexander Craig, and Felix Gilbert. *Makers of Modern Strategy; Military Thought from Machiavelli to Hitler*. Princeton: Princeton University Press, 1943.

Fowler, William M. *Under Two Flags: The American Navy in the Civil War*. 1st ed. New York: Norton, 1990.

Freeman, Douglas Southall. *Lee's Lieutenants, a Study in Command*. New York: C. Scribner, 1942.

Fuller, J. F. C. *The Conduct of War, 1789-1961; a Study of the Impact of the French, Industrial, and Russian Revolutions on War and its Conduct*. New Brunswick, N.J.: Rutgers University Press, 1961.

Gabel, Christopher R. and U.S. Army Command and General Staff College. Combat Studies Institute. *Railroad Generalship*. Fort Leavenworth, Kan.: U.S. Army Command and General Staff College, Combat Studies Institute, 1997.

Gallagher, Gary W. *The Shenandoah Valley Campaign of 1862*. Military Campaigns of the Civil War. Chapel Hill: University of North Carolina Press, 2003.

———. *The Richmond Campaign of 1862 : The Peninsula and the Seven Days*. Military Campaigns of the Civil War. Chapel Hill: University of North Carolina Press, 2000.

Gibson, Charles Dana and E. Kay Gibson. *Assault and Logistics : Union Army Coastal and River Operations, 1861-1866*. Army's Navy Series. Vol. 2. Camden, Me.: Ensign Press, 1995.

Goff, Richard D. *Confederate Supply*. Durham, N.C.: Duke University Press, 1969.

Gragg, Rod. *Confederate Goliath: The Battle of Fort Fisher*. 1st ed. New York: Harper & Row, 1991.

Griffith, Paddy and Paddy Griffith. *Battle Tactics of the Civil War*. U.S. ed. New Haven Conn.: Yale University Press, 1989.

Grimsley, Mark. *The Hard Hand of War: Union Military Policy Toward Southern Civilians, 1861-1865*. Cambridge ; New York: Cambridge University Press, 1995.

Grimsley, Mark and Brooks D. Simpson. *The Collapse of the Confederacy*. Key Issues of the Civil War Era. Lincoln: University of Nebraska Press, 2001.

Hagerman, Edward. *The American Civil War and the Origins of Modern Warfare: Ideas, Organization, and Field Command*. Bloomington: Indiana University Press, 1988.

Harsh, Joseph L. *Confederate Tide Rising: Robert E. Lee and the Making of Southern Strategy, 1861-1862*. Kent, Ohio: Kent State University Press, 1998.

Hattaway, Herman and Archer Jones. *How the North Won: A Military History of the Civil War*. Urbana: University of Illinois Press, 1983.

Hendrick, Burton Jesse. *Lincoln's War Cabinet*. 1st ed. Boston: Little, Brown, 1946.

Hensel, Howard M. *The Sword of the Union: Federal Objectives and Strategies during the American Civil War*. Military History Series. Vol. 87-1. Montgomery, Ala.: Air Command and Staff College, 1989.

Howard, Michael Eliot. *Clausewitz*. Past Masters. Oxford ; New York: Oxford University Press, 1983.

Jomini, Antoine Henri and J. D. Hittle. *Jomini and His Summary of the Art of War;a Condensed Version Edited, and with an Introduction*. Military Classics. Harrisburg Pa.: Washington, Military Service, 1947.

Jones, Archer. *Civil War Command and Strategy: The Process of Victory and Defeat*. New York : Free Press ; Toronto; New York: Maxwell Macmillan Canada; Maxwell Macmillan International, 1992.

———. *The Art of War in the Western World*. London: Harrap, 1988.

Jones, Virgil Carrington. *The Civil War at Sea*. 1st ed. New York: Holt, Rinehart, Winston, 1960.

Leech, Margaret. *Reveille in Washington, 1860-1865*. New York: Time, Inc, 1962.

Lester, Richard I. *Confederate Finance and Purchasing in Great Britain*. Charlottesville: University Press of Virginia, 1975.

Lewis, Emanuel Raymond. *Seacoast Fortifications of the United States; an Introductory History*. Washington: Smithsonian Institution Press, 1970.

Liddell Hart, Basil Henry. *Strategy: The Indirect Approach*. 1st Indian ed. Dehra Dun: Natraj Publishers, 2003.

Livermore, Thomas L. *Numbers & Losses in the Civil War in America, 1861-65*. Civil War Centennial Series. Millwood, N.Y.: Kraus Reprint, 1977.

Lonn, Ella. *Salt as a Factor in the Confederacy*. Southern Historical Publications. Vol. 4. University, Ala.: University of Alabama Press, 1965.

Mahan, A. T. *Letters and Papers of Alfred Thayer Mahan*. Naval Letters Series. Vol. 4. Annapolis: Naval Institute Press, 1975.

———. *Naval Strategy Compared and Contrasted with the Principles and Practice of Military Operations on Land : Lectures Delivered at the U.S. Naval War College, Newport, R.I., between the Years 1887 and 1911*. Westport, Conn.: Greenwood Press, 1975.

———. *The Influence of Sea Power upon History, 1660-1783*. 12th ed. Boston: Little, Brown, 1918.

———. *The Gulf and Inland Waters*. Navy in the Civil War. Vol. 3. New York: Scribner, 1883.

Mahan, A. T. and United States. Marine Corps. *Naval Strategy*. Fmfrp. Vol. 12-32. Washington, DC: U.S. Marine Corps, 1991.

McPherson, James M. *Battle Cry of Freedom: The Civil War Era*. The Oxford History of the United States. Vol. 6. New York: Oxford University Press, 1988.

Meneely, A. Howard. *The War Department, 1861; a Study in Mobilization and Administration*. Studies in History, Economics and Public Law. Vol. 300. New York: Columbia University Press, 1928.

Merrill, James M. *The Rebel Shore; the Story of Union Sea Power in the Civil War*. 1st ed. Boston: Little, Brown, 1957.

———. *The Hatteras Expedition, August, 1861* 1952.

Millis, Walter. *Arms and Men : A Study in American Military History*. New Brunswick, N.J.: Rutgers University Press, 1981.

Musicant, Ivan. *Divided Waters : The Naval History of the Civil War*. 1st ed. New York: HarperCollins Publishers, 1995.

Nevins, Allan. *Ordeal of the Union*. 1st Collier Books ed. New York : $b Collier Books ; Toronto; New York: Maxwell Macmillan Canada; Maxwell Macmillan International, 1992.

Owsley, Frank Lawrence and Harriet Fason Chappell Owsley. *King Cotton Diplomacy: Foreign Relations of the Confederate States of America*. 2nd , rev. ed. Chicago: University of Chicago Press, 1959.

Porter, David D. *The Naval History of the Civil War*. Dover ed. Mineola, NY: Dover Publications, 1998.

Reed, Rowena. *Combined Operations in the Civil War*. Annapolis: Naval Institute Press, 1978.

Roberts, William H. *Now for the Contest: Coastal and Oceanic Naval Operations in the Civil War*. Great Campaigns of the Civil War. Lincoln: University of Nebraska Press, 2004.

Robinson, William M. *The Confederate Privateers*. New Haven; London: Yale University Press; H. Milford, Oxford University Press, 1928.

Roland, Charles Pierce. *The Confederacy*. The Chicago History of American Civilization. Chicago: University of Chicago Press, 1960.

Ropp, Theodore. *War in the Modern World*. Collier Books, BS57. New rev. ed. New York: Collier Books, 1962.

Russel, Robert Royal. *Economic Aspects of Southern Sectionalism, 1840-1861*. Added t.-p.: University of Illinois Studies in the Social Sciences, Vol. 11, Nos. 1 and 2. Urbana: The University of Illinois, 1924.

Sandburg, Carl. *Abraham Lincoln; the War Years* [Abraham Lincoln: the war years.]. New York: Harcourt, Brace, 1939.

Sauers, Richard Allen. *"A Succession of Honorable Victories": The Burnside Expedition in North Carolina*. Dayton, Ohio: Morningside, 1996.

Schwab, John Christopher. *The Confederate States of America, 1861-1865; a Financial and Industrial History of the South during the Civil War*. Burt Franklin Research & Source Works Series, 294. American Classics in History & Social Science. Vol. 54. New York: B. Franklin, 1968.

Sears, Stephen W. *To the Gates of Richmond: The Peninsula Campaign*. New York: Ticknor & Fields, 1992.

Surdam, David G. *Northern Naval Superiority and the Economics of the American Civil War*. Studies in Maritime History. Columbia: University of South Carolina Press, 2001.

Tanner, Robert G. *Retreat to Victory? : Confederate Strategy Reconsidered*. American Crisis Series. Vol. . no. 2. Wilmington, Del.: Scholarly Resources, 2001.

———. *Stonewall in the Valley : Thomas J. "Stonewall" Jackson's Shenandoah Valley Campaign, Spring 1862*. 1st Stackpole , updat and rev ed. Mechanicsville, PA: Stackpole Books, 1996.

Thompson, Samuel Bernard. *Confederate Purchasing Operations Abroad*. Chapel Hill: The University of North Carolina press, 1935.

Todd, Richard Cecil. *Confederate Finance*. Athens: University of Georgia Press, 1954.

Turner, George Edgar. *Victory Rode the Rails; the Strategic Place of the Railroads in the Civil War*. 1st ed. Indianapolis: Bobbs-Merrill, 1953.

Vandiver, Frank Everson, John Tory Bourne, and Smith Stansbury. *Confederate Blockade Running through Bermuda, 1861-1865: Letters and Cargo Manifests*. New York: Kraus, 1970.

Weber, Thomas. *The Northern Railroads in the Civil War, 1861-1865*. New York: King's Crown Press, 1952.

Weigley, Russell Frank. *History of the United States Army*. Enl. ed. Bloomington: Indiana University Press, 1984.

———. *The American Way of War; a History of United States Military Strategy and Policy*. The Wars of the United States. New York: Macmillan, 1973.

———. *Towards an American Army; Military Thought from Washington to Marshall*. New York: Columbia University Press, 1962.

Wesley, Charles H., John David Smith, and Faculty Publication Collection. *The Collapse of the Confederacy*. Southern Classics Series. Columbia, S.C.: University of South Carolina Press, 2001.

West, Richard S. *Mr. Lincoln's Navy*. 1st ed. New York: Longmans, Green, 1957.

Williams, Kenneth P. *Lincoln Finds a General; a Military Study of the Civil War*. New York: Macmillan, 1949.

Williams, T. Harry. *Lincoln and His Generals*. 1st ed. New York: Knopf, 1952.

———. *Lincoln and the Radicals*. Madison: University of Wisconsin press, 1941.

Wise, Stephen R. *Gate of Hell : Campaign for Charleston Harbor, 1863*. Columbia: University of South Carolina Press, 1994.

———. *Lifeline of the Confederacy : Blockade Running during the Civil War*. Studies in Maritime History. Columbia: University of South Carolina Press, 1988.

Published Articles

Anderson, Bern. "The Naval Strategy of the Civil War." *Military Affairs* 26, no. 1 (Spring, 1962): 11-21.

Anderson, Stuart. "1861: Blockade Vs. Closing the Confederate Ports." *Military Affairs* 41, no. 4 (Dec., 1977): 190-194.

Diamond, William. "Imports of the Confederate Government from Europe and Mexico." *The Journal of Southern History* 6, no. 4 (Nov., 1940): 470-503.

Fish, Carl Russell. "The Northern Railroads, April, 1861." *The American Historical Review* 22, no. 4 (Jul., 1917): 778-793.

Grant, U. S. "Military Strategy of the Civil War." *Military Affairs* 22, no. 1 (Spring, 1958): 13-25.

Harsh, Joseph L. "Battlesword and Rapier: Clausewitz, Jomini, and the American Civil War." *Military Affairs: The Journal of Military History, Including Theory and Technology* 38, no. 4 (Dec., 1974): 133-138.

Hattaway, Herman and Archer Jones. "The War Board, the Basis of the United States First General Staff." *Military Affairs* 46, no. 1 (Feb., 1982): 1-5.

James, Joseph B. "Life at West Point One Hundred Years Ago." *The Mississippi Valley Historical Review* 31, no. 1 (Jun., 1944): 21-40.

Johnson, Ludwell H. "Commerce between Northeastern Ports and the Confederacy, 1861-1865." *The Journal of American History* 54, no. 1 (Jun., 1967): 30-42.

Jones, Archer. "Jomini and the Strategy of the American Civil War, A Reinterpretation." *Military Affairs* 34, no. 4 (Dec., 1970): 127-131.

Lebergott, Stanley. "Through the Blockade: The Profitability and Extent of Cotton Smuggling, 1861-1865." *Journal of Economic History* 41, no. 4 (Dec., 1981): 867-888.

Moore, John G. "Mobility and Strategy in the Civil War." *Military Affairs* 24, no. 2, Civil War Issue (Summer, 1960): 68-77.

Morrison, James L., Jr. "Educating the Civil War Generals: West Point, 1833-1861." *Military Affairs* 38, no. 3 (Oct., 1974): 108-111.

Paullin, Charles Oscar. "President Lincoln and the Navy." *The American Historical Review* 14, no. 2 (Jan., 1909): 284-303.

Ropp, Theodore. "Anacondas Anyone?" *Military Affairs* 27, no. 2, Civil War Issue (Summer, 1963): 71-76.

Skelton, William B. "The Commanding General and the Problem of Command in the United States Army, 1821-1841." *Military Affairs* 34, no. 4 (Dec., 1970): 117-122.

Stackpole, E. J. "Generalship in the Civil War." *Military Affairs* 24, no. 2, Civil War Issue (Summer, 1960): 57-67.

Stampp, Kenneth M. "Lincoln and the Strategy of Defense in the Crisis of 1861." *The Journal of Southern History* 11, no. 3 (Aug., 1945): 297-323.

Williams, Harry. "The Attack upon West Point during the Civil War." *The Mississippi Valley Historical Review* 25, no. 4 (Mar., 1939): 491-504.

Williams, T. Harry. "The Return of Jomini--some Thoughts on Recent Civil War Writing." *Military Affairs* 39, no. 4 (Dec., 1975): 204-206.

Appendix A: The "Anaconda Plan"

HEADQUARTERS OF THE ARMY,
Washington, May 3, 1861.
Major General GEORGE B. McCLELLAN,
Commanding Ohio Volunteers, Cincinnati, Ohio:

SIR: I have read and carefully considered your plan for a campaign,* and now send you confidentially my own views, supported by certain facts of which you should be advised.

First. It is the design of the Government to raise 25,000 additional regular troops, and 60,000 volunteers for three years. It will be inexpedient either to rely on the three-months' volunteers for extensive operations or to put in their hands the best class of arms we have in store. The tern of service would expire by the commencement of a regular campaign and the terms not lost be returned mostly in a damaged condition. Hence I must strongly urge upon you to confine yourself strictly to the quota of three-months' men called for by the War Department.

Second. We rely greatly on the sure operation of a complete blockade of the Atlantic and Gulf ports soon to commence. In connection with such blockade we propose a powerful movement down the Mississippi to the ocean, with a cordon of posts at proper points and capture of Forts Jackson and Saint Philip; the object being to clear out and keep open this great line of communication in connection with the strict blockade of the sea-board, so as to envelop the insurgent States and bring them to terms with less bloodshed than be any other plan. I suppose there will be needed from twelve to twenty steam gun-boats, and a sufficient number of steam transports (say forty) to carry all the personnel (say 60,000 men) and material of the expedition; most of the gun-boats to be in advance to open the way, and the remainder to follow and protect the rear of the expedition, &c. This army, in which it is not improbable you may be invited to take an important part, should be composed of our best regulars for the advance and of three-years' volunteers, all well officered, and with four months and a half of instruction in camps prior to (say) November 10. In the progress down the river all the enemy's batteries on its banks we of course would turn and capture, leaving a sufficient number of posts with complete garrisons to keep the river open behind the expedition. Finally, it will be necessary that New Orleans should be strongly occupied and securely held until the present difficulties are composed.

Third. A word now as to the greatest obstacle in the way of this plan- the great danger now pressing upon us-the impatience of our patriotic and loyal Union friends. They will urge instant vigorous action, regardless, I fear, of consequences-that is, unwilling to wait for the slow instruction of (say) twelve or fifteen camps, for the rise of rivers, and the return of frosts to kill the virus of malignant fevers below Memphis. I fear this; but impress right views, on every proper occasion, upon the brave men who are hastening to the support of their Government. Lose no time, while necessary preparations for the great expedition are in progress, in organizing, drilling, and disciplining your three-months' men, many of whom, it is hoped, will be ultimately found enrolled under the call for three-years' volunteers. Should an urgent and immediate occasion arise meantime for their services, they will be the more effective. I commend these views to your consideration, and shall be happy to hear the result.

With great respect, your, truly,

WINFIELD SCOTT.

Appendix B: The Blockade Board's Second Report

Report of a conference in relation to the occupation of points on the Atlantic coast.

WASHINGTON, D. C., July 13, 1861.

Hon. GIDEON WELLES,
Secretary of the Navy:

SIR: We have the honor to inform you that, in further prosecution of the duties assigned ns, we have made a careful study of three of the most important of the secondary bays or harbors on the Southern coast, for the purpose of military occupation. These are Bull's Bay, Saint Helena Sound, and Port Royal Sound, all on the coast of South Carolina. We shall describe each one of them separately, offering some suggestions as to their advantages and the best mode of occupying them, and we will endeavor to explain, by a comparison of their relative merits, the grounds for preferring the two former over the latter for immediate occupation. We have taken them up in the order of their situation from north to south.

Bull's Bay, which has been justly called Noble Harbor of Refuge, is fifteen miles southwest of Cape Romain and twenty-two miles from the main bar of Charleston Harbor. The passage into it is direct, there being but one single course over the bar. The light-house is plainly insight, being less than four miles distant from the outer curve of the bar, and its bearing, together with the soundings and buoys, when properly placed, makes the entrance easy. Twenty feet may be carried in at high water of common tide and fifteen at low water. The channel-way is marked by breakers on either hand, and inside there is a snug, well-protected anchorage in deep water, with good holding-ground. Bull's Bay is situated below the parallel at which the West India hurricanes leave the coast, which very much increases its value as a harbor of refuge. Bull's Island, from which the bay takes its name, is six miles and a half long and about one mile and a half wide. The northeast bluff at the entrance is high and wooded, and admits of being strongly fortified without delay or great expense; but batteries erected to defend the entrance may be taken in the rear by landing about three miles south of the northeast bluff and keeping on the beach till within a mile of the light-house, where a wood road near a fence passes close in the rear of the entire range of sand hills commanding the entrance. It is suggested, therefore, that the extremity of the island should be secured by an in closed work on the point and a line of entrenchments across the island at a distance of two miles, more or less, from the light-house. For defense, Bull's Bay possesses this striking advantage, that it can be held at a single point. Excepting the small sand key (Bird Island),there is no fast land from which it can be attacked. Bird Island is two miles off not easy of access, and insignificant.

It is not probable that any defensive works constructed by the rebels will oppose any formidable obstacle to the occupation of the place, but it is to be considered that its proximity to Charleston subjects it to assault. This assault may be made by combined forces from both
directions, for there is interior water communication with the Santee on the north, as well as with Charleston on the south. Vessels drawing not more than four and a half feet can come out of the Santee through Alligator Creek at the Horns, pass within Cape Island and Raccoon Key, traverse Bull's Bay, and keep inside all the way to Charleston. Very few white men know the whole route, but many negroes are familiar with it. There are six "divides," or places where the tides diverge or converge, between Cape Romain and Charleston Harbor,

Four of these run dry at low water and the other two are encumbered with mud and oyster banks. At this season of the year, however, the rice crops having been carried to market, there is but little intercourse with the Santee district by water. Taking these liabilities into account, it is thought that 4,000 men well intrenched would hold the island, though without an exact knowledge of its topography it is impossible to speak with certainty. The island affords good water, and timber for constructing wharves for coaling, or for other uses, if needed. In these respects, and as a harbor of refuge, there is no point north of Charleston that can be made so useful. It is so easy of access and so perfectly healthy in the hot season that the authorities of Charleston have recommended it for the seat of a quarantine during their strangers' (or yellow) fever months.

The military occupation of Bull's Bay secures the easy command of the four inlets (Price's, Capers', Dewees', and Breach Inlets) lying inter- mediate between it and Charleston Harbor. Neither of these enjoy any trade now, but Dewees' Inlet has seven feet at low water or twelve feet at mean high water, and an. excellent anchorage in four fathoms on the inside. It might prove a useful harbor to vessels of light draft. A deep creek, navigable for boats at low water even to Station Fuller (see chart), enters Dewees' Inlet. From Fuller to Mount Pleasant is nine miles, and it is connected with Hobcaw Point, in rear of Fort Moultrie and Castle Piuckney, for the greater part of the distance, by a well- traveled road in a pine forest. The high road from Charleston to Georgetown, through Christ's Church Parish, passes at an average distance of four miles from the shore. It is well conditioned, the resort of a regular travel, and preserves a communication with the banks of the two Pedees that would suffer no interruption from our occupation of Bull's Island.

Saint Helena Sound, situated nearly midway between Charleston and Savannah, is particularly well adapted to promote the efficiency of the blockading squadron. There are two anchorages, which are healthy throughout the year—one near Otter Island, on the north, and one near Hunting Island, on the south; and the bay is so wide that these two roadsteads may be considered wholly independent of each other. There are three channels of approach—the east, the southeast, and the south channels. The first has only eight feet on the bar at mean low water and fourteen at high; the second, which is a little less direct, has ten and sixteen feet, and the third has seventeen feet at mean low and twenty-three feet at mean high water.

It should be remarked that the month of the South Edisto River is embraced within the northern limits of this sound. The South Edisto is the Edisto proper, the North Edisto being the outlet of the Wadmalaw Sound and the IDawho, while the Edisto itself is a long river, from which large quantities of lumber are sent annually to Charleston. It is navigable for vessels drawing nine feet of water up to Governor Aiken's rice plantation, at Jehosse, where it communicates with North Edisto River through the Dawho. The Dawho is navigable for steamers drawing not more than six feet at all times of tide, under the direction of a pilot. Thirteen feet of water at mean low and nineteen at mean high water can be carried into South Edisto, and there is good anchorage inside, west of Big Bay Island, in five fathoms; but the anchorage on the north side of the bay, which we first mentioned, that under Otter Island, is the better and healthier one of the two.

The continuous ranges of sand shoals, which compose the bar at the several entrances of Saint Helena Sound, extend, unfortunately, six miles to seaward, and the land is low and difficult to distinguish~ the channels, therefore, if used, must be distinctly marked with buoys; the light-ship must be anchored ill a suitable place, and the light-house which has been built on Hunting Island, together with the beacon light near it, must be maintained. Capable pilots must be at hand. The delta shoals in Saint Helena Sound are long and narrow; between them are deep and very regular channels, running in directions nearly parallel to each other, that may be called natural, as regards the rivers of which they are the drains. Beyond these delta shoals a mass of irregular shoals extends out to the southward from Fenwick and Otter Islands (separating South Edisto River from the sound), which, by breaking the sea in easterly storms, preserve comparatively smooth water in the sound. The Ashepoo, Combahee, Bull, Coosaw, Morgan Islands, and Hunting Island (Rivers) empty into the sound. To complete our topographical description we must speak of them in order.

The Ashepoo enters the sound at Otter Island, and at its mouth, under the shelter of the island, is the safe and healthy anchorage we have twice mentioned—safe in all weathers and healthy in all seasons, requiring protection from no other point than Otter Island. Near this anchorage, but separated from it by the delta of the Ashepoo and Coinbahee, is another equally healthy and safe anchorage in six fathoms of water, equidistant between Otter and Morgan Islands, and nearly one and a half nautical miles from each—not easily molested, therefore, from the land, if Otter Island were in our possession.

In crossing the bar and ascending the sound to reach the anchorage a vessel need not approach Hunting Island so near as two miles, or Otter Island nearer than one mile and a half. The Ashepoo is navigable for vessels drawing nine feet of water twelve miles above the point of Otter Island, where they can supply themselves with fresh water on the last of the ebb. Seven miles above is the mouth of Mosquito Creek, which connects with the South Edisto through Bull's Cut.
The light-draft steamers plying on the inland passage from Charleston south go through this cut, descend the Ashepoo, cross the Combahee Bank through a small channel, and thence ascend the Coosaw to Beaufort and Port Royal Ferry. This is only possible for steamers drawing five feet; those of larger draft must pass outside of Otter Island.

We have to penetrate to the depth of six miles into the sound of Saint Helena to reach the point of junction of the Combahee and Coosaw Rivers. The first of these rivers is navigable for vessels drawing ten teet of water some twenty miles up. Fresh water may be had on the ebb about ten miles up. There is a boat connection with the Ashepoo seven miles up. The Coosaw is broader and shoaler than the Combahee; it forms a part of the interior navigation from Charleston. Steamers drawing eight or nine feet will run outside from Charleston to Saint Helena Sound, and entering the latter by the most convenient channel, according to the tide, will proceed up the Coosaw to its junction with Beaufort River at the brick-yard and thence down to Beanfort on the inside way from Savannah and Florida; or the same steamer may continue up Coosaw River to its head, near Port Royal Ferry, and go thence through Whale Branch into Broad River and Port Royal Bay. Vessels bound up the Coosaw may go by the way of Morgami River to Parrot Creek, which connects the two rivers by a 15-foot channel. All these connections are readily traced on a map of a suitable scale. They are pointed out in detail because you will perceive from them how large a tract of country and how extensive, important, and complex a series of lines of interior trade and navigation will be threatened and commanded by the military possession of Saint Helena Sound.

Hitherto we have specified two anchorages as desirable; it remains for us to speak of the third and the best. The south channel, as we have said before, has seventeen feet at low water and twenty-three feet at mean high water; it is therefore quite superior to the others. It leads to an anchorage in five fathoms of water within half a mile of the northeast point of Hunting Island and near the new light-house. Both the anchorage and the adjacent shore are healthy throughout the year. The island is about six miles long, with an average width of little more than half a mile to Johnson's Creek. It is wooded and is stocked with deer, being used as a game preserve. A small creek (Johnson's), with a narrow channel fifteen feet deep near its mouth, runs close to the shore. This is a suitable spot for a coaling depot. There is timber for constructing a wharf, for which there is a natural site near the mouth of a small creek.

We have said that the two anchorages on the north and south sides of the sound are independent of each other. It is so, but the isolation of that which is protected by Hunting Island is the most complete. Here, as in Bull's Bay, and in these two places alone, the military occupation of a single point, remote and inaccessible to a large force except by great expense of time, labor, and money, secures the roadstead, the depot, and the channel of approach; and, in oreover, this channel is the best of the three leading into Saint Helena Sound, from the broader space of which it is effectually separated by a natural barrier of banks, partially (Iry at low water. Neither shells nor solid shot could molest the shipping, nor hardly projectiles from rifled cannon; and the possession of this anchorage commands a considerable extent of inland navigation, though less than that on the north side.

Vessels of heavy draft can pass into Morgan River by turning the spit of a shoal near Hunting Island Point, and those of light draft by an inner channel between Oyster and Egg Banks. Vessels drawing ten feet of water may take an inside passage from Hunting Island to Port Royal Bay, entering the latter through Station Creek. Three points of meeting of the tide occur. The channel is bold in general, but intricate, requiring a pilot. Many wooded hummocks and one large house must be passed within pistol shot. Between Saint Helena Sound and Port Royal Bay are found four inlets—Fripp's, Skull, Pritchard's, and Trenchard's, of which the first and last only, having ten and thirteen feet, respectively, at high water, caii be made available for the uses of commerce.

It is estimated that 4,000 men, in addition to the co-operating naval force, would be sufficient to take and hold Hunting Island, which would be defended, like Bull's Island, by an enclosed work on the point and a line of entrenchments across from the sea to Johnson's Creek at some distance from the light-house. The entrenchments would be less extensive on account of the island being much narrower.

In order to fill out our notes on this vicinity we shall observe that at the eastern end of Saint Helena Island, which forms the right bank of the outlet of Morgan River into Saint Helena Sound, stands the plantation of Mr. Coffin, at whose house commences a public road, called the Sea-side road, that ext ends thirteen miles to Port Royal Bay, at Land's End. Two miles from Mr. Coffin's a road diverges to the right, leading to Ladies Island and Beaufort, distant eleven miles. Both these roads are lined with the residences of gentlemen and sea-island cotton plantations.

Parrot Creek, joining Morgan and Coosaw Rivers, has been referred to. Opposite to it is Village Creek, leading to a village on a bluff; the summer resort of the Saint helena planters. Four fathoms may be carried up Morgan River to Dathaw Island, which is separated from Saint Helena Island by a creek. This creek unites at his head with Cowan Creek, while the latter separates Saint Helena from Ladies Island. Boats pass by this route from Beaufort to Saint Helena Sound. The road to Beaufort from Ashton's, just mentioned, crosses the creek by a bridge at the plantation of the late Mrs. General Eustis. Ladies Island, at the head of Morgan River, is a little more than a mile wide. The town of Beaufort is on the opposite shore of the river of that name. A road leads from Mr. McKee's plantation, at the head of Morgan River, across to the bluff opposite Beaufort.

The above description will enable you to form an idea of the interdependence and of the intercommunication, by boat and carriage, between the islands filling up the head of Saint Helena Sound and the waters emptying into it of the advantages to be derived from its military occupation, and of the opposition, with its means and facilities of combination, which this occupation is likely to provoke.

Port Royal Bay is the finest harbor south of Chesapeake Bay, which it resembles in capacity and extent. It is approached by three channels, the least of which has seventeen feet of water, while the two others have nineteen feet at mean low and twenty-five feet at mean high water. Several of our screw frigates of the first class can pass the bar, and when the entrance is once made a whole navy can ride at anchor in the bay in uninterrupted health and security. The bar, however, is badly situated; the narrowest and shallowest part is so far out from the headlands, which generally furnish natural beacons and sailing-marks, that a conspicuous object is needed on the spot.

The light- ship should be replaced, and large buoys should be planted in proper places (an open screw-pile basket-beacon, well braced, might be put down with great advantage in a well-protected spot, under the lee of Martin's Industry and the southeast breakers). We are looking ahead a little in saying this. The absence of light-vessels, beacons, and buoys will by no means prevent access to the bay. The ships of the expedition will pass through a lane of small vessels anchored on the borders of the natural channel. It is probable that the entrance to the harbor has been fortified on both sides, and especially at Bay Point. This point may be approached in the rear by landing at Pritchard's Inlet, next east of Trenchard's Inlet, near high water, pulling through the creek connecting the two down Trenchard's Inlet to a point near Luce Station, and thence passing along the beach and through the woods to Bay Point. On the Hilton Head side it is more difficult to take the point in the rear. The entrance is over two miles wide~ there is fine anchorage under Bay Point; on the shore there is a number of rough houses, the summer resort of planters. Under the head of Saint Helena we have entered into some details respecting the interior communications and navigation that need not be repeated.

The town of Beaufort, on Port Royal Island, has no commercial importance. During the hot weather, when the planters are in their summer residences, the population numbers about 2,000. At other periods of the year it has but little more than 500 inhabitants. A battery of eight guns, it is said, has been erected at the eastern end of the town. Water may be had at the Station Port Royal, Land's End, Saint Helena Sound, or by sinking wells from six to ten feet deep anywhere along shore, or casks at Bay Point. Near this point may be constructed a wharf for a coaling station above the mouth of the little creek that appears on the Coast Survey chart. The piece of marsh between the fast land and deep water (on the chart) must be crossed by a bridge.
Timber grows close by. The woods directly in the rear of the sea-beach consist chiefly of pine, interspersed with chinquapin and live-oak. Portions of the island are clear and open. Near the beach there are many clumps of myrtle bushes, matted together with jack vines and Cherokee roses. The island is healthy where exposed to the influence of the sea breeze.

Parry's Island, which separates Beaufort and Broad Rivers, is about five miles long, and is devoted to the culture of sea-island cotton. Broad River is navigable up to Charleston and Savannah Railroad station at Pocotaligo. Steamers and sailing vessels from Saint Helena pass round Port Royal Island and enter Broad River by way of Port Royal Ferry and Whale Branch.

Port Royal is one of the wealthiest of the sea islands, and is devoted to the culture of sea-island cotton. Besides this passage of communication between Port Royal Bay and Saint helena Sound through Whale Branch there is a narrow passage, having nine feet at low water, between Lemon and flaw Islands, going down the Chechesee River and entering Skull Creek. A depth of nineteen feet may be carried from Port Royal Bay up Chechesee River to Foot Point, on the Colleton River. This range, a distance of miles, was surveyed in 1859 with reference to a naval depot and coaling station at Foot Point.

Hilton Head Island, which is devoted to the culture of sea-island cotton, extends from Port Royal Bay to Calibogue Sound, and thirteen feet may be carried up the Chechesee, through Skull Creek, to the sound, which constitutes the inland passage to Savannah. The outer shore of Hilton Head Island is so effectually protected by (itaskin Bank and the shoals inside of it, that a landing is practicable in moderate weather. This is facilitated by an inshore channel within the outer breakers.

It may be stated as one general fact, true of the whole coast of South Carolina, that there are from one to two feet less water on the bars during and immediately after westerly gales and as much more during and after northeast and southeast gales. The latter cause the heaviest sea. Another general fact is that those are the most healthy sites which are open to the direct action of the sea breeze. Sheltered points close to the sea-shore will often be unhealthy, while others with a southern exposure six or eight miles inland will be perfectly healthy during the summer and autumn.

For the military occupation of Port Royal Bay it would be necessary, in order to escape molestation. to hold three points, and this would probably involve, as the easiest method of holding them, the occupation of the three islands of which these points form part; that is, Hilton Head Island, Parry's Island, and Phillips' Island. It is difficult to give any precise estimate of the exact number of troops required to hold these islands.

At the present moment, when most of the Southern troops are in Virginia or Tennessee, it is probable that, notwithstanding the contiguity of Savannah and Charleston, no very large bodies could be concentrated against us, but the operation would be likely to withdraw the troops from the north. This effect, almost certain as it is, will compensate us for the application of a considerable force on this point. Six thousand men might take possession of Port Royal, but to hold it permanently would probably require 10,000 or 12,000 men in addition to the available Navy contingent.

Of those three l)laces—BUll's Bay, Saint Helena Sound, and Port Royal Bay—we have no hesitation in recommending the immediate military occupation of the first, for the reasons already fully given in the preceding pages, viz, its accessibility, direct channel, safe anchorage, all of which make it a most convenient harbor of refuge, and its being securely held by the possession of a single point. With regard to Saint Helena Sound and Port Royal Bay there is more room for doubt. We have compared the two somewhat as follows: If Port Royal has the greater depth on the bar (twenty-three to twenty-five feet), yet the bar of the former is eight miles from the land, while that of the latter is only three miles and a half. Saint Helena is held by the occupation of a single point. Port Royal requires that three points should be taken and fortified. The entrance of the former is six miles wide, and the best channel can only be molested from Hunting Island; that of the latter is only two miles wide, and the attacking fleet will be subject to
fire from both sides. The resources for wood and water are about the same in each. Saint Helena is more central between Charleston and Savannah; Port Royal commands a larger interior communication and trade. The noble bay of Port Royal comprises one large open space,
capable of containing any number of vessels anchored in one body. The anchorages of Saint Helena are divided and distinct from each other. It seems to us that Saint Helena ought to be seized before Port Royal, because it will be so much more easily taken and held. The former is a comparatively obscure place, little known and but little resorted to, while the latter is constantly talked of as the first point of attack, and is closely looked after. Stephen Elliott, jr., of Parry's Island, a nephew of George P. Elliott, has been employed in fortifying Port Royal, every foot of which he is familiar with, while not a planter knows Saint Helena.

Finally, believing that the three points we have recommended will suffice for the purposes of coaling stations and harbors of refuge for the blockading squadrons, we are not disposed to recommend any immediate measures for the taking of Port Royal. The putting of 12,000 or 15,000 men thus in the immediate neighborhood of Charleston and Savannah and the presence of a considerable fleet in this noble harbor would doubtless be a sore annoyance to the rebels, and necessitate the constant maintenance of large forces in those cities and on those shores. Yet the same force, naval and military, organized as an expedition and held in hand at New York for a blow anywhere, would threaten not only Savannah and Charleston, but the whole Southern coast.

If, in the organization of such a force, its destination should be absolutely undefined, the threat would be equally against every important point of the Southern coast from Hatteras to the Rio Grande. The simple putting to sea of such a force, if it were only to return to its port, would cause general alarm, and the Gulf States could no longer permit their troops to swell the armies of Virginia. '11 he force thus organized, after being, by frequent embarkations and disembarkations, used as a means of threat, and thus perfectly drilled to its intended service, might at last be permitted to strike its blow. Whether at New Orleans, or Mobile, or Pensacola, or Savannah, or Port Royal, or that focus of rebellion—the scene of the great indignity offered our flag—Charleston, might be decided at the last moment.

We have the honor to be, very respectfully, your obedient servants

S.F. PU PONT,
Captain, U. S. Navy, President.
A. D. BACHE,
Superintendent U. S. Coast Survey.
J. G. BARNARD,
Major, U. S. Engineers.
CHAS. H. DAVIS,
Commander, U. S. Navy, Secretary.

Appendix C: McClellan to Lincoln, Aug 2, 1861

The object of the present war differs from those in which nations are usually engaged mainly in this, that the purpose of ordinary war is to conquer a peace and make a treaty on advantageous terms. In this contest it has become necessary to crush a population sufficiently numerous, intelligent, and warlike to constitute a nation. We have not only to defeat their armed and organized forces in the field, but to display such an overwhelming strength as will convince all our antagonists, especially those of the governing, aristocratic class, of the utter impossibility of resistance. Our late reverses make this course imperative. Had we been successful in the recent battle (Manassas), it is possible that we might have been spared the labor and expenses of a great effort.

Now we have no alternative. Their success will enable the political leaders of the rebels to convince the mass of their people that we are inferior to them in force and courage, and to command all their resources. The contest began with a class; now it is with a people. Our military success can alone restore the former issue.

By thoroughly defeating their armies, taking their strong places, and pursuing a rigidly protective policy as to private property and unarmed persons, and a lenient course as to private soldiers, we may well hope for a permanent restoration of a peaceful Union. But in the first instance the authority of the Government must be supported by overwhelming physical force.

Our foreign relations and financial credit also imperatively demand that the military action of the Government should be prompt and irresistible.

The rebels have chosen Virginia as their battle-field, and it seems proper for us to make the first great struggle there. But, while thus directing our main efforts, it is necessary to diminish the resistance there offered us by movements on other points both by land and water.

Without entering at present into details, I would advise that a strong movement be made on the Mississippi, and that the rebels he driven out of Missouri.

As soon as it becomes perfectly clear that Kentucky is cordially united with us, I would advise a movement through that State into Eastern Tennessee, for the purpose of assisting the Union men of that region, and of seizing the railroads leading from Memphis to the East. The possession of those roads by us, in connection with the movement on the Mississippi, would go far towards determining the evacuation of Virginia by the rebels. In the mean time all the passes into Western Virginia from the East should be securely guarded, but I would advise no movement from that quarter towards Richmond, unless the political condition of Kentucky renders it impossible or inexpedient for us to make the movement upon Eastern Tennessee through that State. Every effort should, however, be made to organize, equip, and arm as many troops as possible in Western Virginia, in order to render the Ohio and Indiana regiments available for other operations.

At as early a day as practicable it would be well to protect and reopen the Baltimore and Ohio Railroad. Baltimore and Fort Monroe should be occupied by garrisons sufficient to retain them in our possession.

The importance of Harper's Ferry and the line of the Potomac in the direction of Leesburg will be very materially diminished so soon as Our force in this vicinity be- comes 6rganized, strong, and efficient, because no capable general will cross the river north of this city when we have a strong army here ready to cut off his retreat.

To revert to the West: It is probable that no very large additions to the troops now in Missouri will be necessary to secure that State.

I presume that the force required for the movement down the Mississippi will be determined by its commander and the President. If Kentucky assumes the right position, not more than

20,000 will be needed, together with those that can be raised in that State and Eastern Tennessee, to secure the latter region and its railroads, as well as ultimately to occupy Nashville.

The western Virginia troops, with not more than 5,000 to 10,000 from Ohio and Indiana, should, under proper management, suffice for its protection.

When we have reorganized our main army here 10,000 men ought to be enough to protect the Baltimore and Ohio Railroad and the Potomac; 5,000 will garrison Baltimore, 3,000 Fort Monroe, and not more than 20,000 will be necessary at the utmost for the defense of Washington.

For the main army of operations I urge the following composition:

	Men.
250 regiments of infantry, say	225,000
100 field batteries, 600 guns	15,000
28 regiments of cavalry	25,500
5 regiments engineer troops	7,500
Total	273,000

The force must be supplied with the necessary engineer and pontoon trains, and with transportation for everything save tents. Its general line of operations should be so directed that water transportation can be availed of from point to point by means of the ocean and the rivers emptying into it. An essential feature of the plan of operations will, be the employment of a strong naval force, to protect the movement of a fleet of transports intended to convey a considerable body of troops from point to point of the enemy's sea-coast, thus either creating diversions and rendering it necessary for them to detach largely from their main body in order to protect such of their cities as may be threatened, or else landing and forming establishments on their coast at any favorable places that opportunity might offer. This naval force should also co-operate with the main army in its efforts to seize the important seaboard towns of the rebels.

It cannot be ignored that the construction of railroads has introduced a new and very important element into war, by the great facilities thus given for concentrating at particular positions large masses of troops from remote sections and creating new strategic points and lines of operations.

It is intended to overcome this difficulty by the partial operations suggested, and such others as the particular case -may require. We must endeavor to seize places on • the railways in the rear of the enemy's points of concentration, and we must threaten their seaboard cities, in order that each State may be forced, by the necessity of its own defense, to diminish its contingent to the Confederate army.

The proposed movement down the Mississippi will produce important results in this connection. That advance and the progress of the main army at the East will materially assist each other by diminishing the resistance to be encountered by each.

The tendency of the Mississippi movement upon all questions connected with cotton is too well understood by the President and Cabinet to need any illustration from me.

There is another independent movement that has often been suggested, and which has always recommended itself to my judgment. I refer to a movement from' Kansas and Nebraska through the Indian Territory upon Red River and Western Texas, for the purpose of protecting and developing the latent Union and free-State sentiment well known to predominate in Western Texas, and which, like a similar sentiment in Western Virginia, will, if protected, ultimately organize that section into a free State. How far it will be possible to support this movement by an advance through New Mexico from California is a matter which I have not sufficiently examined to be able to express a decided opinion. If at all practicable it is eminently desirable, as bringing into play the resources and warlike qualities of the Pacific States, as well as identifying them with our cause and cementing the bond of union between them and the General Government.

If it is not departing too far from my province, I will venture to suggest the policy of an intimate alliance and cordial understanding with Mexico; their sympathies and interests are with us—their antipathies exclusively against our enemies and their institutions. I think it would not be difficult to obtain from the Mexican Government the right to use, at least during the present contest, the road from Guaymas to New Mexico. This concession would very materially reduce the obstacles of the column moving from the Pacific. A similar permission to use their territory for the passage of troops between the Panuco and the Rio Grande would enable us to throw a column of troops by a good road from Tampico, or some of the small harbors north of it, upon and across the Rio Grande, without risk, and scarcely firing a shot.

To what extent, if any, it would be desirable to take into service and employ Mexican soldiers is a question entirely political, on which I do not venture to offer an opinion.

The force I have recommended is large; the expense is great. It is possible that a smaller force might accomplish the object in view, but I understand it to be the purpose of this great nation to re-establish the power of its Government and restore peace to its citizens in the shortest possible time.

The question to be decided is simply this: Shall we crush the rebellion at one blow, terminate the war in one campaign, or shall we leave it as a legacy for our descendants?

When the extent of the possible line of operations is considered, the force asked for the main army under my command cannot be regarded as unduly large; every mile we advance carries us farther from our base of operations and renders detachments necessary to cover our communications, while the enemy will be constantly concentrating as he falls back. I propose, with the force which I have requested, not only to drive the enemy out of Virginia and occupy Richmond, but to occupy Charleston, Savannah, Montgomery, Pensacola, Mobile, and New Orleans; in other words, to move into the heart of the enemy's country and crush the rebellion in its very heart.

By seizing and repairing the railroads as we advance the difficulties of transportation will be materially diminished. It is, perhaps, unnecessary to state that, in addition to the forces named in this memorandum, strong reserves should be formed, ready to supply any losses that may occur. In conclusion, I would submit that the exigencies of the Treasury may be lessened by making only partial payments to our troops when in the enemy's country, and by giving the obligations of the United States for such supplies as may there be obtained.

[1] Du Pont to Goldsborough, 9 Nov 1861. *Samuel Francis Du Pont; a Selection from His Civil War Letters*, ed. John D. Hayes, Vol. I, *The Mission: 1860-1861*; Vol. II, *The Blockade: 1862-1863*; Vol. III, *The Repulse: 1863-1865* (Ithaca, N.Y.: Cornell University Press published for the Eleutherian Mills Historical Library, 1969), Vol. I, p. 229. Cited hereafter as *SFDP Letters*

[2] Welles to Du Pont, 16 Nov 1861. *SFDP Letters*, Vol. I, p. 246. Also see, *Official Records of the Union and Confederate Navies in the War of the Rebellion*. (Washington: Government Printing Office, 1894-1922) Ser. I, 12, p. 290. Cited hereafter as *ORN*.

[3] J.F.C. Fuller, *The Conduct of War, 1789-1961; a Study of the Impact of the French, Industrial, and Russian Revolutions on War and its Conduct*. (Rutgers University Press, 1961), p. 101. Fuller labeled the Union's failure to seize Wilmington earlier in the war a "first rate blunder." Also see, Theodore Ropp, *War in the Modern World*. (New York: Collier Books, 1962), p. 190-191. Ropp correctly opined that the most efficient and full proof way to "plug the leaks in the blockade" would have been for the Union to have simply captured the ports. The Confederacy's ten principal seafaring ports consisted of Norfolk, New Bern, Wilmington, Charleston, Savannah, Jacksonville, Fernandina, Pensacola, Mobile, and New Orleans. Herman Hattaway and Archer Jones, *How the North Won: A Military History of the Civil War*. (Urbana: University of Illinois Press, 1983), p. 127.

[4] Gary W. Gallagher. "Blueprint for Victory," in James McPherson and William J. Cooper Jr., eds., *Writing the Civil War: The Quest to Understand*. (Columbia: Univ. of South Carolina Press, 1998), p. 32. Prior to Gallagher's observations, the standard works covering the Navy's role in the conflict were James, Merrill's *The Rebel Shore; The Story of Union Sea Power in the Civil War*. (Little, Brown, 1957), and Bern Anderson's *By Sea and by River: The Naval History of the Civil War* (New York: Knopf, 1962). Since Gallagher's comments, several pieces of quality scholarship have emerged. See William Fowler's *Under Two Flags: The American Navy in the Civil War* (New York: Norton, 1990), Ivan Musicant's *Divided Waters: The Naval History of the Civil War* (New York: HarperCollins, 1995), and William Roberts thought provoking, scholarly, and concise macro history *Now for the Contest: Coastal and Oceanic Naval Operations in the Civil War* (Lincoln: University of Nebraska Press, 2004). Of the recent works, however, the efforts of Robert Browning clearly stand out. Browning authored *From Cape Charles to Cape Fear: The North Atlantic Blockading Squadron during the Civil* (Tuscaloosa: University of Alabama Press, 1993) and *Success is all that was Expected: The South Atlantic Blockading Squadron during the Civil War* (Washington, D.C.: Brassey's, Inc., 2002). None of these exceptional scholars, however, placed the planning and conduct of naval operations within the larger context of the Union war effort. Their conclusions regarding the untapped strategic potential of the Union Sea Service were reached at the end of studies focused strictly on the Navy. In Browning's case, his scholarly and superbly researched works were, nonetheless, even further restricted to the specific activities of a particular blockading squadron.

[5] Specific examples of the Union's overwhelming advantage in strategic mobility include the embarkation and waterborne transportation of the Army of Potomac, approximately 121,000 men, from Washington to Fort Monroe in the spring of 1862 and the overland rail movement of the Union corps XI and XII corps, totaling some 25,080 men, from Virginia to Tennessee in the wake of the Union's stunning defeat at Chickamauga. See, Stephen W. Sears, *To the Gates of Richmond: The Peninsula Campaign*. (New York: Ticknor & Fields, 1992), p. 24 and Christopher R. Gabel, *Railroad Generalship*. (Fort Leavenworth, Kan.: U.S. Army Command and General Staff College, Combat Studies Institute, 1997), p. 6. For Confederate dependence on blockade running and logistics see Stephen R. Wise, *Lifeline of the Confederacy : Blockade Running during the Civil War*. S (Columbia: University of South Carolina Press, 1988) and Richard Goff's classic work, *Confederate Supply*. (Durham, N.C.: Duke University Press, 1969). For a concise summary of the historiography regarding the blockade and its effectiveness see David G. Surdam, "The Union Navy's Blockade Reconsidered," *Naval College Review*, Autumn 1988, Vol. LI, No. 4.

[6] Scott to McClellan, 3 May 1861. *The War of the Rebellion: A Compilation of the Official Records of the Union and Confederate Armies*, 128 vols. (Washington: Government Printing Office, 1880-1901) Ser. I, 51, pt. I, p. 369. Cited hereafter as OR. Scott's famous letter, actually written as a tactful rebuff to an ill-advised strategic proposal submitted by McClellan, remains the most concise primary source document explaining the General-in-Chief's strategic views. For McClellan's initial proposal see McClellan to Scott, 27 April 1861. OR, Series I, 51, pt. I, pp. 338-339.

[7] Ibid., p. 370.

[8] Gideon Welles, *The Diary of Gideon Welles, Secretary of the Navy under Lincoln and Johnson.* (Boston, Houghton Mifflin, 1911), Vol. I, p. 242. Cited hereafter as *The Diary of Gideon Welles*.

[9] Diary entry dated 17 August 1862. Welles, *The Diary of Gideon Welles*, Vol. I, pp. 83-86.

[10] Welles, *Diary of Gideon Welles*, Vol. I, pp. 10-11. Welles, at least initially, appears to have underestimated both the nature and strength of the rebellion. In this regard he was not alone. Lincoln's Post Master General, Montgomery Blair, viewed the rebellion as nothing more than a small group of "armed marauders" who could be easily put down: "It would require but a very inconsiderable part of the forces at our command to put down this band of plunderers, if used vigorously, and as soon as they are put down, the deliverers will be welcomed in Virginia, as they are now in Maryland." Blair to Massachusetts Gov. John Andrew, 11 May 1861; quoted in Nevins, *The Improvised War*, pp.150-151. Blair's naïve illusions of Union troops being greeted as liberators in Virginia reflected the overoptimistic political assumptions, regarding both the nature and strength of the rebellion that clouded the judgment of many political leaders in Washington, including the President, during the initial months of the war. As late as July 4, 1861, the President told Congress, "It may well be doubted whether there is, today, a majority of the legally qualified voters of any State, except perhaps South Carolina, in favor of disunion. There is much reason to believe that the Union men are the majority in many, if not in every other one, of the so-called seceded States." Lincoln to Congress, 4 July 1861. *The Collected Works of Lincoln*, 9 vols., ed. Roy P. Basler (New Brunswick, N.J.: Rutgers University Press, 1953–55), Vol. IV, p. 437. Cited hereafter as, *The Collected Works of Lincoln.*

[11] For divergent theoretical views of naval strategy and the application of sea power see Alfred Thayer Mahan, *Naval Strategy Compared and Contrasted with the Principles and Practice of Military Operations on Land : Lectures Delivered at the U.S. Naval War College, Newport, R.I., between the Years 1887 and 1911.* (Westport, Conn.: Greenwood Press, 1975) and Julian Corbet, *Some Principles of Maritime Strategy* (London; New York: Longmans, Green, 1918).

[12] Eads to Welles, 29 April 1861. ORN, Series I, 22, pp. 278-279. As early as April 1861, the Navy made plans and preparations to support Scott's drive down the Mississippi. On April 29, Welles received a letter from James B. Eads, one of the nation's leading river engineers, outlining a plan for blockading the commerce of the seceding States along the Mississippi watershed. Eads emphasized the strategic importance of Cairo, Illinois and further advocated that it should become the primary base of operations for sealing the Mississippi.

[13] Welles to Cmdr John Rodgers, 14 May 1861. ORN, Series I, 22, p. 280. Welles's instructions clearly defined the command relationship between the two services. "You will proceed to Cincinnati, Ohio, or the headquarters of General McClellan, where [ever] they may be, and report to that officer in regard to the expediency of establishing a naval armament on the Mississippi and Ohio rivers, or either of them, with a view of blockading or interdicting communication and interchanges with the States that are in insurrection. This interior non intercourse is under the direction and regulation of the Army, and your movements will therefore be governed in a great degree by General McClellan, the officer in command, with whom you will put yourself in immediate communication. He will give such orders and requisitions as the case to him shall seem necessary, you acting in conjunction with and subordinate to him." See also Cameron to McClellan, 14 May 1861. ORN, Series I, 22, p. 279.

[14] Though not specifically stated in the parlance of modern military vernacular, Scott's Anaconda created two military theaters of operations and established a supporting/supported command relationship in each one. Welles rapidly reorganized the department to conform with the Navy's paramount strategic tasking-the establishment and maintenance of the blockade. On May 1, he appointed Flag Officer S.H. Stringham commander of the newly created Atlantic Blockading Squadron. The Secretary followed that announcement, less than a week later, by naming Flag Officer Mervine to command the squadron assigned to blockade the Gulf coast. The organization and functioning of the overburdened department was also greatly improved by Lincoln's appointment of Gustavas Fox to become the Chief Clerk of the Navy Department on May 8, 1861. Welles to Fox, 8 May 1861 in *Confidential Correspondence of Gustavus Vasa Fox: Assistant Secretary of the Navy, 1861-1865,* 2 vols., ed. Robert Thompson and Louis H. Bolander (New York: Printed for the Naval history society, 1918)., Vol. I, p. 45. Cited hereafter as *Fox Correspondence.* For concise accounts of the Navy's role in the development of Union military strategy see, Kevin J. Weddle, "The Blockade Board of 1861 and Union Naval Strategy," *Civil War History*, Vol.

48, no. 2, and Bern Anderson, "The Naval Strategy of the Civil War." *Military Affairs* 26, no. 1 (Spring, 1962), pp. 11-21.

[15] Welles originally wanted the Army's Chief Engineer, Joseph G Totten, to serve on the board. See, Fox to Du Pont, 22 May 1861. *SFDP Letters*, Vol. I, p. 71. Though Totten's duties precluded his participation, Major Barnard, an up and coming and extremely talented young officer, who also happened to be one of Winfield Scott's aides, became the Army representative on the board. See, Welles to Barnard, 26 June 1861. ORN, Series I, 12, p. 196. Du Pont, one of the most respected and professionally accomplished naval officers in the department, was a natural choice to serve as the senior naval officer on the board. Though initially lukewarm to the idea, he came to fully embrace both the necessity and the potential of the endeavor. Du Pont's Mexican War experience gave him keen operational insights on the task ahead. See Du Pont to Bache, 30 May 1861. *SFDP Letters*, Vol. I, p. 74. For an overview of the board and its role in the development of Union naval strategy see, Bern Anderson, "The Naval Strategy of the Civil War" *Military Affairs* Vol. 26, No. 1 (Summer 1963), pp. 11-21. Anderson was the first historian to label the naval board as "The Strategy Board." Care, however, must be taken not to exaggerate the board's importance on the one hand, nor minimize it on the other. While Anderson credits Welles's commissioning of the four member board as an innovative step that, in effect, established the first "joint" planning staff, Kevin Weddle argued the formation of the board may have had more to do with old fashion Yankee capitalism and bureaucratic self interest rather than any sublime strategic vision on Welles's part. Weddle opines that Bache, as the director of the Coast Survey, initiated the board in an effort to justify and preserve his department. See, Weddle, "The Blockade Board of 1861 and Union Naval Strategy," p.127. A detailed examination of the board's activities, however, indicates that the truth is much more complex, and lies somewhere in the middle. Evidence supports the view that Bache was the principle catalyst behind the board's inception. And while, the board was originally conceived to examine and make recommendations on the selection and seizure of coaling stations in support of the blockade, it nonetheless, expanded and evolved its charter over time. While the board reports focused on tactical and operational details of executing the blockade, the reports also produced innovative and progressive strategic thought and recommendations.

[16] Weddle, "The Blockade Board of 1861 and Union Naval Strategy," *Civil War History*, Vol. 48, no. 2, p. 134.

[17] First report of conference for the consideration of measures for effectively blockading the South Atlantic Coast, 5 July 1861. ORN, Series I, 12, p. 196. The board wrote, "We separate in our minds the two enterprises of a purely military expedition and an expedition the principal design of which is the establishment of a naval station for promoting the efficiency of the blockade."

[18] Ibid., p. 198. The board concluded, "Finally, we will repeat the remark made in the beginning of this report that we think this expedition to Fernandina should be undertaken simultaneously with a similar expedition having a purely military character."

[19] Report of conference for the consideration of measures for effectively blockading the South Atlantic Coast, 13 July 1861. OR, Series I, 53, p. 72. The board clearly envisioned the potential of expeditionary operations, or the threat thereof, to draw off Confederate troops then hastening north, "At the present moment, when most of the Southern troops are in Virginia or Tennessee, it is probable that, notwithstanding the contiguity of Savannah and Charleston, no very large bodies could be concentrated against us, but the operation would be likely to withdraw the troops from the north."

[20] Ibid., p. 73. The report also noted "If, in the organization of such a force, its destination should be absolutely undefined, the threat would be equally against every important point of the Southern coast from Hatteras to the Rio Grande. The simple putting to sea of such a force, if it were only to return to its port, would cause general alarm, and the Gulf States could no longer permit their troops to swell the armies of Virginia. The force thus organized, after being, by frequent embarkations and disembarkations, used as a means of threat, and thus perfectly drilled to its intended service, might at last be permitted to strike its blow. Whether at New Orleans, or Mobile, or Pensacola, or Savannah, or Port Royal, or that focus of rebellion—the scene of the great indignity offered our flag—Charleston, might be decided at the last moment."

[21] Ibid.

[22] Du Pont to Mrs Du Pont, 26 July 1861. *SFDP Letters*, Vol. I, p. 111. Du Pont wrote, "two expeditions will go at once and pounce upon two ports little suspected and watched." His initial belief in both the

immediacy and locations of the pending operations, however, proved short lived. Welles, however, shrewdly used the board's initial reports to draw attention to the urgent requirement for undertaking two expeditionary operations in order to establish coaling stations for the blockading squadrons. Having obtained the first objective, the department used the process to foster the type of inter-service cooperation necessary to procure the troops the Navy needed to seize and guard them. By routing the reports through the General-in-Chief, they not only gained his support, but also demonstrated the type of professional courtesy and coordination necessary for effective inter-service cooperation.

[23] Du Pont to Mrs Du Pont, 28 July 1861 and Du Pont to Mrs Du Pont, 1 Aug 1861. *SFDP Letters*, Vol. I, pp. 116-117.

[24] Du Pont to Mrs Du Pont, 1 Aug 1861. *SFDP Letters*, Vol. I, p. 117. Du Pont originally advocated an earlier date in order to mitigate the risk of an Atlantic hurricane to the naval shipping. The General pointed out, however, that the health of the troops would be jeopardized by an early September landing in the brackish waters and sultry climate along the southeastern coast. This point was not lost on Du Pont, who later remarked, "Mosquitoes are worse than Minie balls."

[25] Ibid.

[26] Thomas Scott to Sherman, 2 Aug 1861. OR, Ser. I, 6, p. 168.

[27] In July 1813, Scott embarked 200 men aboard the *General Pike*, and executed a series of amphibious raids against British supply depots along the coast of Lake Erie. During the Blackhawk War, Scott transported 800 regulars, 6 companies of mounted rangers, and the entire 1832 class of West Point 1800 miles from Fort Monroe, VA to Chicago in just 18 days. The most remarkable example of Scott's comprehension of expeditionary operations remains the organization and landing at Vera Cruz. See Peskin, *Winfield Scott and the Profession of Arms*, pp. 32-33, 83, 145-152. The board members clearly envisioned the creation of a large expeditionary force designed to operate against or threaten the Confederacy's major port cities. See, OR, Series I, 53, pp. 72-73.

[28] The final two board reports were completed on July 26 and August 9 respectively. The fourth report dealt almost exclusively with the coast of Georgia, while the final report focused on the Gulf of Mexico and New Orleans.

[29] Du Pont to Fox, 29 Sept 1861. *SFDP Letters*, Vol. I, p. 158. Du Pont lamented, "we have one paper unfinished, which to us as individuals, and to the Department for convenience, it is most desirable to finish. It is the recapitulation or summary of our whole work, to furnish the basis of instructions to the different squadrons, while it will be the most attractive to the general reader. The large memoirs will attest our research, the summary will show the results-and complete the archives of the Department on a subject which will do honor to it hereafter."

[30] Those that argue the board played a major influence on the strategic direction of the war must also keep in mind that many of its most important findings were ignored or dramatically altered. For example, the board strongly cautioned against a naval attack on New Orleans. See Naval Board Report # 5, entitled "First report of conference for the consideration of measures for effectually blockading the coast bordering on the Gulf of Mexico," 9 August 1861. ORN, Ser. I, Vol. 16, p. 627. The report cautioned "We regard its conquest as incompatible with the other nearer and more urgent naval and military operations in which the Government is now and will be for some time hereafter engaged. It is an enterprise of great moment, requiring the cooperation of a large number of vessels of war of a smaller class, but of formidable armament, a great many troops, and the conduct of sieges, and it will be accomplished with slow advances." Fox, however, disregarded the board's recommendations and played a major role in engineering the naval *coup de main* that seized the South's most important city. Many of the board's ideas, especially those pertaining to larger combined operations, threatened Fox's control and conflicted with his vision of the Navy Department's role in determining the outcome of the war. While Fox was vindicated by Faragut's remarkable success at New Orleans, his failure to allow the board to complete its work in the fall of 1861 was a missed opportunity. A final report that integrated the various, and often competing, activities of the three separate blockading squadrons, and the various military departments under a common strategic direction or operational umbrella would have proved invaluable. This was a job, however, that Fox, undoubtedly, thought he could, or should do himself.

[31] Welles to Stringham, 17 July 1861. ORN, Ser. I, 6, pp. 6-7. Also see, Crea to Fox, 29 May 1861. *Fox Correspondence*, Vol. I, p. 359. Even prior to the Army's the disaster at Manassas, powerful voices within

the Northeastern commercial shipping industry had turned impatience, unrealistic expectations, and an imperfect understanding of military reality into loud admonishments directed at the administration regarding the inefficiency of the blockade. Just three weeks into his tenure as Chief Clerk of the Navy, Gustavus Fox received a letter describing, "the growing discontent created in the public mind by the extraordinary and disheartening delays of the Navy Department." The complaint promised "meetings of the People, who will declare their want of confidence," and concluded with the remarkable admonishment that "A month has elapsed since the Blockade proclamation… [yet] every Port, south of the Chesapeake… is still open." Another particularly irate businessman scolded the Secretary of State: "Why can not those ports named be blockaded? God knows there are steamers enough in this country—guns, men, and materials enough to close them up as tight as a bottle." On the day after Bull Run, Welles forwarded still more complaints to Stringham about Confederate privateering off the North Carolina coast. Welles to Stringham 22 July 1861. ORN, Ser.I, 6, p. 27. This initial criticism, even if it reflected a certain amount of ignorance, affected Fox and Welles deeply. Both men had strong personal connections to the Northeast, and both were very concerned about the public image and reputation of the department.

[32] NY Board of Underwriters to Welles, 12 Aug 1861. ORN, Ser. I, 6, pp. 77-80. The reports warned that the Confederates were in the process of erecting fortifications along the coast. The business men also took the opportunity to remind Welles of the "large number of vessels with valuable cargoes, which, in the usual course of navigation, pass in the vicinity of Cape Hatteras," and concluded with the strong recommendation that "it is greatly to be desired that immediate steps be taken by the Government to prevent, as far as possible, any further captures by the pirates who sally out from those inlets."

[33] Scott to Wool, 13 Aug 1861. OR, Ser. I, 4, p. 579.

[34] Ibid.

[35] Wool to Scott, 24 Aug 1861. OR, Ser. I, 4, p. 603. Wool and his naval counterpart, Flag Officer Stringham, lacked situational awareness regarding the naval board and the larger strategic direction of the war even then just beginning to take shape in Washington. Both men, however, echoed the naval board's recommendations for the creation of a large expeditionary force, and also clearly envisioned the potential employment of large-scale expeditionary operations along the southern coasts in pursuit of strategic objectives.

[36] It was aboard the USS *Minnesota,* anchored off of Fort Hatteras on the North Carolina coast, a full six months before the events of Forts Henry and Donelson, that Flag Officer Stringham and General Butler, not U.S. Grant, first offered the now famous terms of "Unconditional Surrender" to capitulating Confederate forces. For The terms of capitulation see Butler to Barron, 29 Aug. 1861. OR, Ser. I, 4, p. 583.

[37] Butler's Hatteras Report, 30 Aug 61. OR, Ser. I, 4, pp. 581-586.

[38] Browning, *From Cape Charles to Cape Fear*, p. 14. Most historians credit the expedition for seizing a staging base for Burnside's subsequent operations in eastern North Carolina the following year. See James Merrill, "The Hatteras Expedition, August, 1861." North Carolina Historical Review 29 (April 1952), p. 218. Viewed in the larger context of the Union war effort, however, the success of the expedition may have inadvertently set the stage for an incremental application of expeditionary force in eastern North Carolina that depleted limited Union resources and hindered long term strategic objectives.

[39] Butler's Hatteras Report, 30 Aug 61. OR, Ser. I, 4, pp. 581-586. Butler described his rationale for the decision, "On consultation with Flag-Officer Stringham and Commander Stellwagen I determined to leave the troops and hold the fort, because of the strength of the fortifications, its importance, and because, if again in the possession of the enemy, with a sufficient armament, of the very great difficulty of its capture, until I could get some further instructions from the Government." He also noted: "The importance of the point cannot be overrated. When the channel is buoyed out any vessel may carry 15 feet of water over it with ease. Once inside, there is a safe harbor and anchorage in all weathers. From there the whole coast of Virginia and North Carolina, from Norfolk to Cape Lookout, is within our reach by light-draught vessels, which cannot possibly live at sea during the winter months. From it offensive operations may be made upon the whole coast of North Carolina to Bogue Inlet, extending many miles inland to Washington, New Berne, and Beaufort. In my judgment, it is a station second in importance only to Fortress Monroe on this coast. As a depot for coaling and supplies for the blockading squadron it is invaluable. As a harbor for our coasting trade, or inlet from the winter storms or from pirates, it is of the first importance."

[40] Davis to Cobb, 31 August 1861. ORN, Ser. I, 6, p. 137.

[41] *Petersburg Express* (Petersburg, VA) quoted in Merrill, "The Hatteras Expedition, August, 1861," p. 205. One Raleigh resident commented, "The whole eastern part of the State is now exposed to the ravages of the merciless vandals… It is now plunged into a great deal of trouble."

[42] Browning, *From Cape Charles to Cape Fear*, p. 20. The public apprehension created in North Carolina and throughout the South can be ascertained by a review of the regions newspapers. Merrill cites the following primary sources as evidence of the "panic" created by the Hatteras seizure: Charleston Mercury, The Daily Richmond Examiner, September 2, 1861; Newbern Progress, quoted in the Sacramento Daily Union, October 1, 1861. For additional background see Richard Sauers, *"A Succession of Honorable Victories": The Burnside Expedition in North Carolina*. (Dayton, Ohio: Morningside, 1996).

[43] The official title of McClellan's new command was yet to be determined. See General Orders 47, 25 July 1861. OR, Ser. I, 2, p. 763. "The Department of Washington and the Department of Northeastern Virginia will constitute a geographical division, under Major-General McClellan, U. S. Army; headquarters, Washington." Upon McClellan's arrival it was subsequently named the Division of the Potomac until its formal re-designation as the Army of the Potomac. The confusion about where this command, and McClellan himself, fit in to the existing Union military table of organization led to the rift between Scott and McClellan, and adversely effected the development of Union military strategy during the first eighteen months of the war.

[44] The circumstances surrounding the McClellan-Scott feud are well known, yet the strategic consequences of the confrontation remain underappreciated. The most succinct summary is Mark Grimsley, "Overthrown: The Truth Behind the McClellan-Scott Feud," *Civil War Times Illustrated* 19 (Nov. 1980), pp. 20-29.

[45] McClellan to Lincoln, 2 Aug, 1861. Stephen Sears, ed., *The Civil War Papers of George B. McClellan*, pp. 71-72. The document, prepared and delivered at the President's request, afforded McClellan the opportunity to work directly with the President, thereby circumventing the General-in-Chief. McClellan's strategic concept was remarkably Clausewitzian. It focused on the destruction of the Confederate armies by the application of decisive and overwhelming force. McClellan, also, clearly identified the Southern center of gravity as the planter elite and aristocratic class that he believed was leading, financing, and inspiring the insurrection. While bemoaning the premature commitment of force at Bull Run, he now viewed the struggle as essentially a people's war. Though McClellan expressed concern about maintaining the rights and property i.e. slaves, of southern non-combatants, this was consistent with the law of war at the time, and almost certainly done in an effort to prevent the conflict from degenerating into the type of costly and indecisive guerilla war that had bogged Napoleon down in Spain. T. Harry Williams flatly dismissed McClellan's plan. He called it "defective in almost every respect. It was fundamentally wrong because it proposed to concentrate the military effort in one theater to the neglect of the others and because it would have made places instead of enemy armies the objectives." See T. Harry Williams, *Lincoln and His Generals*. (New York: Knopf, 1952), pp. 30-31. For perspective on Williams's interpretation see Liddel Hart, *Strategy: The Indirect Approach*, pp. 126-136. Hart argued that Sherman's March to the Sea was the decisive campaign of the war and that it was aimed at places, not the destruction of the rebel army. Sherman achieved the latter, indirectly, by destroying Confederate manufacturing and attacking Southern moral. For additional analysis of McClellan's strategic thinking see, Joseph Harsh, "George Britton McClellan and the Forgotten Alternative: An Introduction to the Conservative Strategy of the Civil War: April-August 1861." Ph.D. diss., (Rice University, 1970). pp. 185-226. Cited hereafter as *"McClellan and the Forgotten Alternative."*

[46] Comparing the differences between Scott's and McClellan's strategic thinking, Gideon Welles observed in 1863 "The anaconda policy was, I then thought and still think, unwise for the country. The policy of General McClellan has not been essentially different." See Welles, *The Diary of Gideon Welles, Secretary of the Navy under Lincoln and Johnson*, Vol. I, p. 242.

[47] McClellan to Lincoln, 2 Aug, 1861. Sears, ed., *The Civil War Papers of George B. McClellan*, p. 71.

[48] Ibid. McClellan wrote, "An essential feature of the plan of operations will, be the employment of a strong naval force, to protect the movement of a fleet of transports intended to convey a considerable body of troops from point to point of the enemy's sea-coast, thus either creating diversions and rendering it necessary for them to detach largely from their main body in order to protect such of their cities as may be threatened, or else landing and forming establishments on their coast at any favorable places that opportunity might offer. This naval force should also co-operate with the main army in its efforts to seize

the important seaboard towns of the rebels." For a sympathetic interpretation of McClellan's amphibious ambitions see, Rowena Reed's, *Combined Operations in the Civil War*. (Annapolis: Naval Institute Press, 1978), p. xvii. Reed stated "Had McClellan's brilliant strategy been fully implemented it would have ended the Civil War in 1862, as intended." Reed's work has assumed a rather influential place in the historiography of the war. It remains the best, and coincidentally, the only, scholarly study focused on expeditionary operations. She argued that combined operations held the key to Union success and that McClellan, had he not been thwarted, would or could have used them to achieve victory. Unfortunately, rather than focusing on a strict assessment of how or why the use of combined operations held so much promise, she became distracted with a lengthy defense of McClellan's generalship at almost every turn. Her strong endorsement of McClellan, put her at odds with the vast majority of her collogues, and, at times, was certainly overblown.

[49] Scotts Resignation Letter to Cameron 9 Aug 1861. OR. Ser. I, 11, pt..3, p. 4.

[50] Townsend to Sherman, 14 Sept 1861. OR, Ser. I, 6, p. 171. On September 14, Scott was forced to recall Sherman, who was then in New York busily preparing his troops for the pending campaign: "Come here with all your command without delay, leaving the smallest guard necessary to protect your camp." On the following day, Scott relayed the news to Du Pont. He reluctantly told the flag officer that the expedition was postponed because of the "panic" about the security of Washington and the subsequent requirement to withhold Sherman's troops to bolster the capital's defenses. Du Pont to Mrs Du Pont, 15 Sept 1861. *SFDP Letters*, Vol. I, p. 147. Summarizing the day's frantic activities, Du Pont, simply noted "I believe this place is quite secure, yet they get such exaggerated reports of the numbers of the rebels that they will never stop reinforcing here." Du Pont immediately sought confirmation from the Navy Department. Both Fox and Welles echoed the bad news, but assured Du Pont that the expedition would go forward.

[51] McClellan to Lincoln, 2 Aug , 1861. Sears, ed., *The Civil War Papers of George B. McClellan*, p. 73. McClellan predicated any use of expeditionary forces on the condition that they were employed with, or directly in support of, the "main army." Furthermore, he envisioned a sequential, almost methodical, series of operations that would only take place after he had fought his Napoleonic battle of annihilation on the outskirts of Richmond, and had in fact seized the enemy's capital.

[52] Du Pont to Mrs. Du Pont, 17 Sept 1861. *SFDP Letters*, Vol. I, p. 149. Lincoln not only reversed his early decision at the cabinet meeting on the September 17, but according to Du Pont, actually hastened the expedition's departure, "the President has directed that the expedition go forward *coute que coute*, and indeed his vehemence has run into another extreme, for he declares it must sail in *ten* days." On September 18, Lincoln formally approved the Port Royal expedition. Lincoln to Cameron, 18 Sept 1861. OR, Ser. I, 6, p. 171. The President clearly sensed the necessity to bring some clairvoyance to the situation when he wrote, "To guard against misunderstanding I think fit to say that the joint expedition of the Army and Navy, agreed upon some time since, and in which General T. W. Sherman was and is to bear a conspicuous part, is in nowise to be abandoned, but must be ready to move by the 1st of or very early in October. Let all preparations go forward accordingly." On the same day, the Navy Department, acting in accordance with the naval board's original recommendations, reorganized the Atlantic Blockading Squadron into two separate commands. The reorganization was facilitated by Flag Officer Stringham's convenient request to be relieved, which Welles accepted without hesitation. See Welles to Stringham 18 Sept 1861 ORN, Ser. I, 6, pp. 231-32. Flag Officer Goldsborough was placed in command of the Northern Blockading Squadron, while Du Pont assumed responsibility for the Southern Blockading Squadron. Welles to Goldsborough 18 Sept 1861. ORN, Ser. I, 6, pp. 233-34. For Du Pont's orders to take command of the newly created South Atlantic Blockading Squadron, see Welles to Du Pont 18 Sept 1861. *SFDP Letters*, Vol. I, p. 152.

[53] Du Pont to Henry Du Pont, 15 Oct 1861. *SFDP Letters*, Vol. I, p. 164. Du Pont commented, "This expedition has grown like a mushroom, much beyond the original intentions and therefore raising undue expectations-so that the points originally intended will seem insignificant, I fear, to the proportions it has assumed. I think of attacking Port Royal though I hear of their having two hundred guns there." The board originally recommended the seizure of Bulls Bay, South Carolina and Fernandina, Florida. It considered Port Royal too formidable an objective Though Welles delegated the final decision to Du Pont, Fox had other designs. He felt the expedition's objective should be Port Royal. Fox visited Du Pont in Hampton Roads on October 22. See Du Pont to Mrs. Du Pont, 23 Oct 1861. *SFDP Letters*, Vol. I, pp. 180-182. Fox departed the morning of October 23, and was not in attendance at the final planning conference held later that evening. Even before Fox's arrival, Du Pont was unsettled. See Du Pont to Mrs. Du Pont, 17 Oct 1861.

SFDP Letters, Vol. I, pp. 170-71. "There is no question that Port Royal is the most important point to strike, and the most desirable to have first and hold, yet we did not think so in our conference and I must weigh well before I deviate." He also saw the selection of Port Royal as a vital lodgment for follow on operations, "Port Royal alone admits the large ships-and gives us such a naval position on the sea coast of the enemy as our army is holding across the Potomac." For insight into Fox's influence on the final decision see Du Pont to Mrs. Du Pont, 17 Oct 1861. *SFDP Letters*, Vol. I, p. 171, n. 7, "Fox, who later met with SFDP at Hampton Roads, persuaded him to take Port Royal, probably for the reason stated here. On a letter from SFDP referring to "the *big* place," Fox noted: "Port Royal, that I insisted upon." (SFDP to Fox, 24 Oct. 1861, Fox Papers, NY Historical Society). See also Du Pont to Fox 24 Oct 1861. *Fox Correspondence*, I, p. 58.

[54] For a description of the meeting and a summation of Du Pont's concerns see Du Pont to his wife 23 & 24 Oct 1861 *SFDP Letters*, Vol. I, pp. 182-184.

[55] Du Pont to Fox 24 Oct 1861. *Fox Correspondence*, I, p. 58. The letter also seemed intended to manage expectations and convey the Army's reservations. "A long and earnest conference last night with the Generals was followed by another this morning on the practicability of the *big* place. The necessity of occupying those points as stated in our memoirs on it & the extreme doubt I am sorry to say, on a closer look of getting this ship over the bar gave gravity not to say anxiety to the council-but I am happy to say that they all came in & we are about decided Sherman & I, to try. But I tell you it is a much greater job than you & I contemplated-the landing of troops an reserves to be brought by the enemy from Savannah & Charleston may be great embarrassments-I wish you could have been with us."

[56] Du Pont to Fox, 29 Oct 1861. *SFDP Letters*, Vol. I, p. 199. For an exact listing of the ships see, "Order of Sailing, Port Royal Expeditionary Corps and Fleet," *SFDP Letters*, Vol. I, p. 203.

[57] Lee's Department stretched from Charleston to Fernandina, Florida.

[58] Douglas Southall, Freeman. *R. E. Lee, a Biography*. (New York: Scribner, 1934), Vol. I, p. 608. Initially, Confederate authorities assumed the citizens of South Carolina and Georgia would quickly rally to defend their respective states, but the much-anticipated ground swell of volunteers failed to materialize. Lee's manpower problems were not confined to numbers alone, more critical, perhaps, was the lack of trained artillerist to man the guns. See Lee to Benjamin. OR, Ser. I, 6, p. 335 and Lee to Cooper, 21 Nov 1861. OR., p. 327.

[59] Lee to Cooper, 21 Nov 1861. OR, Ser. I, 6, p. 327. Lee wrote "The guns from the less important points have been removed, and are employed in strengthening those considered of greater consequence. The entrance to Cumberland Sound and Brunswick and the water approaches to Savannah and Charleston are the only points which it is proposed to defend. At all of these places there is much yet to be done, but every effort is being made to render them as strong as the nature of the positions and the means at hand will permit."

[60] Lee to Cooper, 8 Jan 1862. Ibid., p. 367.

[61] Ibid.

[62] Sherman to Thomas, 14 December 1861. Ibid., pp. 203-204. Sherman correctly ascertained both the nature and intent of the Confederate dispositions: "The object of this line appears to be to resist an invasion of the main-land, and not to attack the occupied coast, which, from all that can be learned, the enemy have concluded they cannot maintain, and given up all idea of doing so." Du Pont concurred with Sherman's assessment, observing, "The enemy have left the coast defenses they put up and have fallen back on their rail roads for their base." See Du Pont to Whetten, 28 Dec 1861. *SFDP Letters*, Vol. I, pp. 292-93.

[63] H.W. Davis to Du Pont, 15 Nov 1861. Ibid., p. 245.

[64] Du Pont to James Wilson Grimes, 2 Dec 1861. *SFDP Letters*, Vol. I, p. 269. Du Pont, echoing both Davis's sentiments and the recommendations of the second board report wrote, "I wish I could speak to you of the operations contemplated by the Army here, but I do not know the plan of campaign. But I will venture an opinion, that if they move without preponderating numbers, it will be the same old story."

[65] Du Pont to Whetten, 28 Dec 1861. *SFDP Letters*, Vol. I, pp. 292-93. As early as December 2, 1861 Du Pont observed "the inland waters of South Carolina and Georgia connecting through both states to Florida? They offer great facilities to reach the capitals of these states, which *must* be taken. Armed boats and launches could give great protection, and cover crossing the streams, etc.-like the wonderful expeditions of

the Spaniards in Holland so finely described by Motley." See, Du Pont to James Wilson Grimes, 2 Dec 1861. *SFDP Letters*, Vol. I, p. 269

[66] Du Pont, however, clearly envisioned both the potential and the fleeting opportunity see, Du Pont to Morgan, 24 Dec 1861. *SFDP Letters*, Vol. I, p. 285. "The occupation of this wonderful sheet of water, with its tributary rivers, inlets, outlets, entrances and sounds, running in all directions, cutting off effectually all water communications between Savannah and Charleston, has been like driving a wedge into the flanks of the rebels between these two important cities."

[67] Sherman to Thomas, 14 December 1861. OR, Ser. I, 6, pp. 203-204.

[68] Ibid, p. 204.

[69] Ibid.

[70] Du Pont to Fox, 11 Jan 1862. Ibid., pp. 100-101.

[71] See McClellan to Lincoln, Aug 2, 1861. Sears, ed., *The Civil War Papers of George B. McClellan*, pp. 71-75, McClellan to Cameron, 6 Sept 1861. OR, Ser. I, 5, pp. 586-87, and McClellan to Burnside, 7 Jan 1862, in Sears, ed., *Civil War Papers of George B. McClellan*, pp. 148-49. McClellan envisioned the use of expeditionary forces to cooperate and assist his own army as he marched down the eastern seaboard, not to be used independently in pursuit of strategic objectives. Though he had taken the rather innovative step of creating Burnside's amphibious division, he clearly intended that it remained under his own operational control and in support of his pending move on Richmond.

[72] McClellan's initial enthusiasm for combined operations waned considerably upon the stark realization that troops for such expeditions would be drawn from his own army. See, McClellan to T. Scott, 17 Oct 1861. OR, Ser. I, 6, p. 179. McClellan complained, "It is the task of the Army of the Potomac to decide the question at issue. No outside expedition can effect the result. I hope that I will not again be asked to detach anybody."

[73] Du Pont to Whetten, 28 Dec 1861. *SFDP Letters*, Vol. I, pp. 292-93.

[74] Ibid., p. 294. The stories drew several angry responses from Du Pont who quipped "our people and press should be patient with the General, they have had to be long time patient with others who have had relatively much greater means to the end. Expeditionary corps in Europe are always "*hommes d'elite*"; the best regiments from the Potomac should have been sent."

[75] McClellan to Sherman, 6 Mar 1862. OR, Ser. I, 6, p. 238. McClellan's orders were indecisive "If it will not interfere with any operation of greater importance that you may now have on hand, the General-in-Chief hopes that you will be able to arrange with Commodore Du Pont for the prompt occupation of Fernandina, in accordance with the original plan of the expedition. It is supposed that this operation will not interfere with the reduction of Fort Pulaski, which is regarded as a matter of very great importance." Though both operations succeeded, Sherman eventually became a causality of McClellan's own demise in Washington, and was relieved of his command on April 3, 1862. Du Pont was not happy about Sherman's relief. Though both men were clearly frustrated, personal relations between the two military professionals remained amicable. Du Pont wrote the general a sincere and heartfelt letter praising his "vigorous and harmonious cooperation." Du Pont also noted the general's "unflagging zeal with which you have availed yourself of every means in your power to secure an effective tenure of this coast while preparing a base of operations which, with the reinforcements you had a right to look for, would have led to more brilliant but in no manner more important results than those you have accomplished." Du Pont to Sherman, 3 April 1862. ORN, Ser. I, 12, p. 701. Sherman responded in kind "our intercourse and cooperation have been of the most perfect harmony, and of this I am proud, and all I regret is that I have never had the material and the means to afford that assistance in our combined operations that would have been productive of the most good to the service and most agreeable to myself." Sherman to Du Pont 3 Apr 1862. ORN, Ser. I, 12, p. 702. Sherman's replacement, Major General David Hunter wasted little time recalling the army's troops from Florida. He told Stanton "It is my opinion that this force is entirely too much scattered and is subject to be cut off in detail." The new commander concluded with his intent was to. "hold the Savannah River with a small force and to concentrate on Charleston." Hunter to Stanton, 3 April 1862. OR, Ser. I, 6, pp. 263-64.

[76] Stephen Wise, *Lifeline of the Confederacy: Blockade Running during the Civil War*. (Columbia: University of South Carolina Press, 1988), p. 226. Wise wrote that "In terms of basic military necessities, the South imported at least 400,000 rifles, or more than 60 percent of the nation's modern arms. About three million

pounds of lead came through the blockade, which by Gorgas's estimate amounted to one-third of the Army's requirements. Besides these items, over 2,250,000 pounds of saltpeter, or two-thirds of this vital ingredient for powder, came from overseas. Without blockade running the nation's military would have been without proper supplies of arms, bullets, and powder. Blockade running also supplied countless other essential items such as food, clothing, accoutrements, chemicals, paper, and medicine." Stephen Wise concluded, "By the summer of 1862, the flow of supplies enabled the Confederate armies to stand up to the numerically superior Federals. Because of the work of the men involved in blockade running, a supply lifeline was maintained until the very last months of the war."

[77] Seddon to Davis, 10 Dec 1864. Ibid., p. 930.

[78] While the Civil War is generally considered America's first modern war, some historians remain strangely naive to the vital role of logistical difficulties played on the Confederate war effort. See for example, Beringer, Hattaway, Jones, and Still, *Why the South Lost the Civil War*, p. 9. "The fact is, no confederate army lost a major engagement because of the lack of arms, munitions, or other essential supplies."

[79] Gorgas to Seddon, 13 Oct 1864. ORA, Ser. IV, 3, p. 733. 1,507,000 pounds of lead, 1,933,000 pounds Saltpeter, 545,000 Boots and shoes, 8,632,000 pounds of meat, 69,000 rifles, and 520,000 pounds of coffee had been imported through the ports of Wilmington and Charleston between November 1, 1863 and December 10, 1864.

[80] Fuller, *The Conduct of War*, p. 101. See also Hattaway and Jones, *How the North Won*, p. 127.

[81] It may be of interest to note that the War Department spent 2.7 Billion dollars during the conflict. This represented nearly nine times the 314 million spent by the Navy during the same period. Davis Dewey, *The Financial History of the United States*. 12th ed. (New York, 1936), p. 329.

[82] Fox to Goldsborough, 9 Nov 1861. *Fox Correspondence*, I, 203.

[83] Ibid., pp. 92-93. Historians have been quick to dismiss Scott's strategic concept out of hand, but as Joseph Harsh so aptly pointed out, "No one has even shown that Northern impatience was irresistible, or that Scott's plan could not at least have been tried. To what extent, it might be asked, would impatience have impaired moral? Would a bloodless strategy have dampened Northern morale more than the casualty lists of the Wilderness battles? Would Scott's way have been more frustrating or more depressing than Grant's? One should recall the decline of Northern morale in the late summer of 1864 before assuming these questions are easily disposed of."

[84] By the summer of 1862 the Army of Northern Virginia became the embodiment of Southern martial prowess and the will to resist.

[85] Charles Roland, *The Confederacy*. (Chicago: University of Chicago Press, 1960), p. 195. Roland reminds us that the Confederacy eventually mustered nearly a 1,000,000 southern men into military service. More than one fourth of these men would die from wounds or disease. If viewed as a percentage of total population, Southern losses were nearly equivalent to those suffered by the major European powers during the two greatest blood lettings of the Twentieth Century. If the North would have suffered a similar percentage, Union war dead would have totaled somewhere around a 1,000,000 instead of 300,000, the colonies in their struggle with England would have lost 94,000 killed instead of 12,000, and the United States would have suffered 6,000,000 war dead instead of 300,000 during the Second World War.

[86] Walter Mills, *Arms and Men: A Study in American Military History*. (Rutgers University Press, 1981). p. 48

[87] Harsh, "Battlesword and Rapier," p. 137. This was Harsh's principle argument which seems to have been inspired by C Van Woodward, "Equality: America's Deferred Commitment," *The American Scholar*, XXVII (Autumn, 1958), pp. 459-460.

Figure 1: Major Expeditionary Operations of the American Civil War
Source: Source: USMA History Department. Available online at
http://www.dean.usma.edu/history/web03/atlases/AtlasesTableOfContents.html

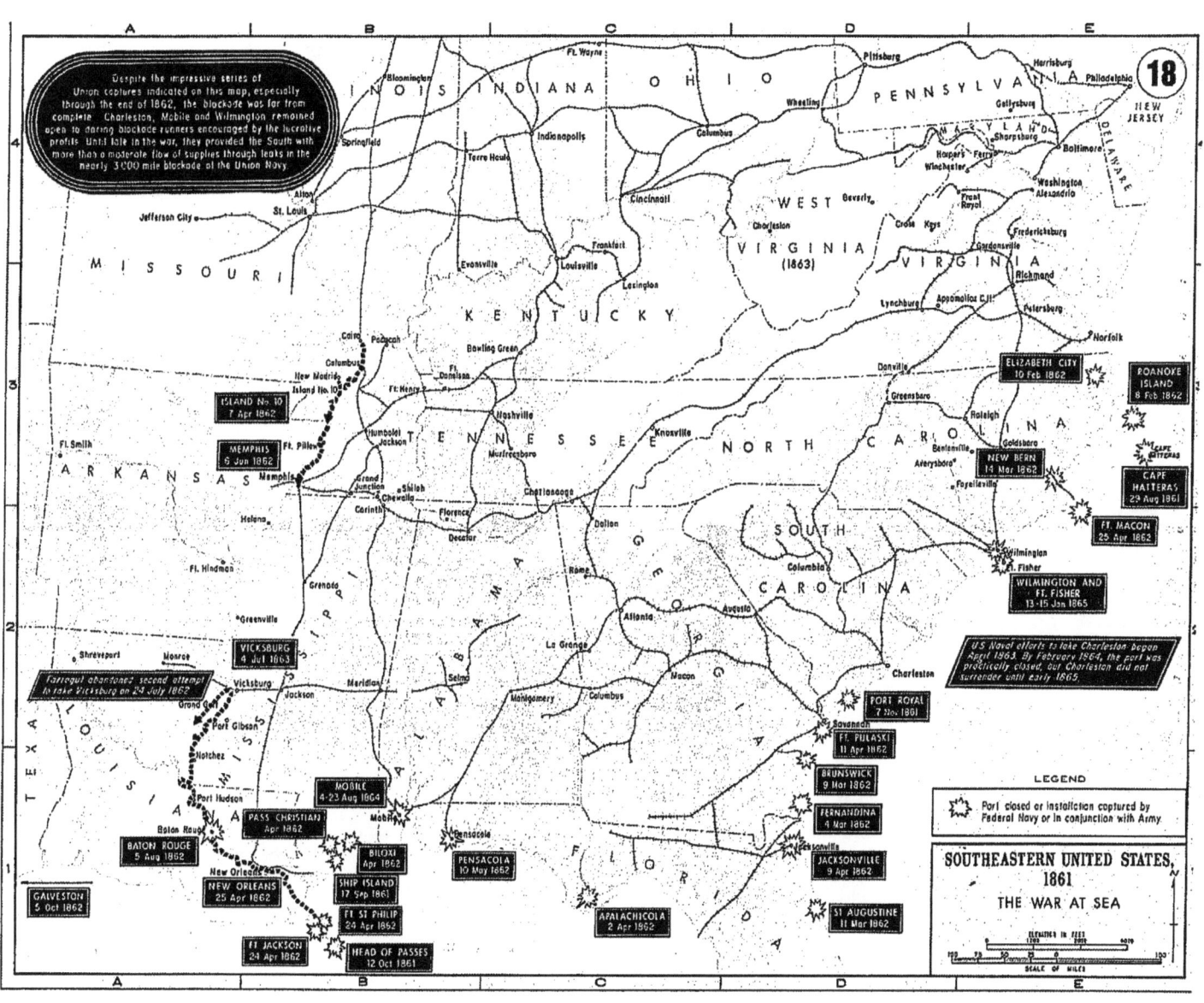